Dream Medicine

Dream Medicine

The Intersection of Wellness and Consciousness

KIMBERLY R. MASCARO

Toplight

Jefferson, North Carolina

ISBN (print) 978–1-4766–8743–8
ISBN (ebook) 978–1-4766–4512–4

LIBRARY OF CONGRESS AND BRITISH LIBRARY
CATALOGUING DATA ARE AVAILABLE

Front cover illustration by Elena Faenkova (Shutterstock)

Printed in the United States of America

Toplight is an imprint of McFarland & Company, Inc., Publishers

*Box 611, Jefferson, North Carolina 28640
www.toplightbooks.com*

This book is dedicated to many.
It is dedicated to those who dream.
This book is also dedicated to all healers,
especially healthcare professionals worldwide.
Last but not least, this book is dedicated
to my naturopathic and holistic health care team.

Table of Contents

Table of Contents

Disclaimer

THIS BOOK OFFERS personal stories, research findings, and specific techniques for enhancing wellness by accessing nonordinary/higher states of consciousness and incorporating practices into your life. These are not substitutes for professional counseling, psychotherapy or medical advice, including psychiatry. If you have any physical or mental health concerns, consult your doctor or other medical professional. The author and publisher assume no responsibility or liability for the actions of the reader.

Acknowledgments

THIS BOOK WOULDN'T BE POSSIBLE without the support of a very large group of caring people. Thank you to my agent John White and the entire team at McFarland and Toplight. A very special thanks to Dr. Stanley Krippner for his ongoing support in so many areas of my life and for his insights and advice related to this work. Additional thanks go to Dr. Kristin Sorensen, a long-time friend, colleague and editor of my work. I am also very grateful to those colleagues who shared their ideas and insights through conversation or formal interview, helping and guiding this process immensely. In addition, I want to acknowledge and honor those who have dedicated their lives to conducting research, providing treatment, and offering education in alternative medicine and indigenous healing traditions. It's not easy doing this in today's for-profit, conventional world. I also want to express deep gratitude to my wonderful friends in California and across the globe who offered feedback throughout the process and even prayed and dreamed on my behalf. A special thanks to my family and partner for believing in my dreams (*actually taking the time to listen to them*) and for trusting my process. Last but not least, I want to thank the International Association for the Study of Dreams. The IASD Board of Directors along with other members of this professional dream organization offered hope and support at levels beyond what I imagined. I am grateful. Grazie tutti!

Preface

CONSCIOUSNESS, THE VASTNESS of extraordinary human potentials, takes us beyond space and time. I have always valued dreams and all that dream-like states have to teach. In these so-called altered states of consciousness, we are not bound but free. It wasn't until the last couple of years that my faith in these phenomena took a huge leap forward. A lot has happened during the writing of this book, *Dream Medicine*. When what some call Source, God, the Divine, or Creator wants someone to wake up, to heal her life, the message can be heard loud and clear, if we are listening, tuning in. This was recorded in my dream journal, August 2019:

> *I am viewing a scene from above and also from the back (of the room). I'm either two people simultaneously or witnessing the two people. But were these even people? One body or being is feathered. The other is covered in skin like a reptile—it could be a snake skin. The feathered body has a wound: either an injury or cut on the left rib area. Some feathers are missing there. The scene is a spiritual or divine courthouse. There are pews like in a church, but this place also has a feeling of being in court for divine negotiation/judgment. Does my rib need aid? I'm wondering. The negotiations taking place involve some thoughts or decisions about others … about me—the sense of something taking place related to some aspect of divinity is in the forefront of my mind as the dream ends.*

Now let's fast forward a couple of months and let me tell you a little more about what went on over here, in my world. It was a pleasant California day in October 2019 and I had been awaiting an important call. Surely I'd hear from the doctor today or tomorrow at the latest. I had a task ahead of me, now that the most recent public safety power outage had come to an end. I drove to the fairgrounds to begin setting up a large-sized shrine dedicated to deceased family members—the 20th annual Altar Show was expected to open to the public the next day now that the town's power was restored. I arrived at the site, unloaded my two tables, an oversized tablecloth and framed family photographs, and I began to set up. I'm now midway though the process of completing the shrine's construction when finally I am able to connect with the doctor. She tells me it's not good and gives the more official name. I pace and nod, while knowing she can't see me. "OK," I say, "thanks for letting me know." I gather a few more details and slip in a question before we hang up the phone: "As far as diet goes, what should I avoid?" Knowing that what we eat can have an impact as far as disease progression versus prevention goes, I felt bewildered that this was not mentioned ... not during any of my 2018 or 2019 appointments and not even when I was given the diagnostic information. Nor was the benefit of increasing exercise mentioned. I had to push for this kind of information. *Was this typical?* I wondered. I didn't expect a conventional medical doctor to ask me about my intuitive hunches, emotional troubles, or my dreams, but no mention of diet and exercise? Really?

From that moment, I knew that if I was going to get well it was up to me. I could not relinquish my power. I could not faithfully wait around for anyone to save me. Whether my physical body would heal was and is unknown, but I knew that I held the power within myself to heal my relationship with my spirit and my soul. Taking responsibility for treating this condition meant I had to act on multiple levels. I had my dreams, my intuition, the ability to use visualization, meditation, protective charms, and prayer, for starters. If prevention or empowerment is of little interest to the conventional medical community, then that meant I had to reach out, ask to be freshly educated, get out of my head, and accept my role in healing. So I did.

All year long, I intuitively knew that I needed to exercise more and eat healthier. Off and on, I did just that. But it wasn't a prioritized daily lifestyle routine. I had recorded my nocturnal and waking dreams rather faithfully, and while important messages surfaced, I did not take the messages in deeply enough to prompt great change in the way I lived. They were communicating, but I wasn't really listening.

Once I decided to take a front seat in the vehicle for change, a new pathway revealed itself to me. More dreams, even synchronistic events, were undeniable. Some of what I will share I was already accustomed to or had some experience with, such as special diets or health routines. Anyone at any age can make these changes and embark on these practices. Some people claim to be "too old" to make changes, but I believe *now* is always the best time. There are no absolute prerequisites. So, from then on, several daily practices became part of my new way of being. The first new way was adopting an organic whole food plant-based diet. When I needed motivation, I read books about naturopathic therapies and metabolic theories, visited websites such as radicalremission.com, pcrm.org and nutri tionfacts.org for health inspiration or watched health documentaries on Netflix. I wanted to be informed. The second new way of being has been ensuring that I get 30 minutes or more of daily movement—exercise in any form. The third way has been following Donna Eden's daily energy medicine routine. Fourth, 30–60 minutes of some form of meditation each day: anything from mindful walking to guided meditation to a concentrative breathing-focused sitting practice to a prayerful Ho'oponopono ritual (this one was very new to me). Fifth was visualization with intention, often supported through self-hypnosis. For example, on some days I choose to breathe in my personal healing color filling the body while mentally stating, "My body is a healing temple. My body is functioning optimally right now." Then I breathe out the color of the illness. On some days, I feel moved to use Ho'oponopono to apologize to my body for ignoring its needs and for taking this on in the first place. I envision the unhealthy cells finding a new home after transforming into something higher. Sixth, I made gratitude lists and reminded myself of all the good reasons to live. I even used magazine scraps to construct a vision board reflecting only healing imagery. Sometimes I painted. Seventh, I continued to record my dreams, but more frequently, and gave them a higher status when it came to health-related choices and decision-making. I was rewarded with more lucidity than I had had for quite some time and my shamanic journeying practice became stronger. In addition, I considered making career and work-related changes where I could. And finally, because I decided to invest money in alternative healing modalities once I believed I was worth it, I hired two naturopathic doctors and a licensed acupuncturist, among others in the helping and healing professions. This may seem like a lot, and it really felt that way at first. My life did a 180. Some days I was overwhelmed. Then, as the months passed by, it became easier and more natural. This new way of life wasn't so terrible. I was at a crossroads and had important decisions to make. Everything I have stated above has been *my own personal choice* due to my belief system and what I had access to. It might be the wrong choice for someone else so I make no claims nor do I advise anyone to do what I did or continue to do since the ride isn't over yet. I can only share my stories and experiences and some of my life with you here. Maybe someone will find it helpful. My desire is to inspire creativity, courage and hope—to give people a boost and remind them that they are not alone.

In thinking more about my list of practices above, I'd like to add that I had to be sure to stay in the moment as much as possible, since once these activities became more routine, the easier it was to do them on automatic pilot. Beware of this pitfall. Moment-to-moment conscious awareness and grounding has positive impacts for reducing tension (that can come along with a diagnosis) and also for intuitive development. After all, the "sleep-walking" of autopilot does nothing for nervous system regulation or the powers of intention. We can direct our energy for our benefit in the waking state and the dream state, so stay calmly vigilant and aware as much as possible. Yes, this is all easier said than done. I know. While we may feel scrambled or scattered at first, it is imperative to find a balanced, sustainable health routine since this is a marathon, not a sprint.

Because this book is about what I like to call *dream medicine*— meaning any health-related practice outside of the faster brain wave waking states—let's return to discussing altered-state healing, or health-promoting activities from nonordinary states of consciousness (altered state, an older term, and nonordinary state will be used interchangeably throughout this book). That is using dreams (including dream reentry), shamanic journeys, meditation or prayer, visions, trance, and embodied intuitive knowing to take ownership of our health and capacity for self-healing. I propose that we must heal our spirit first so that our physical manifestation (the body) can follow. In essence, this book surveys a broad landscape. It is my hope that this book brings to light some of the possibilities of our human potentials along the path of becoming your own wellness guide.

Earlier I mentioned diet and exercise. Harnessing the brilliance of a well-functioning system requires that we clean it regularly. Avoiding alcohol, staying hydrated, and consuming organic produce is one way. Energizing energy and blood flow via movement is another way. There are many more. Yes, it is true, what we eat and drink and what we do (food and exercise) directly impacts our dreams, our memory systems, our moods, our ability for clarity during hypnotic or trance states, our ability to focus during meditation, and more. When we give ourselves the best fuel, our potential to heal and transform and our inherent internal power multiplies. I'm just telling it like it is.

A couple weeks after getting the diagnosis, I'm at home when I hear a scream coming from outside. I look out the window and see what appears to be a car wreck. I put on warmer clothes (a long sweater, socks and boots) and go out to investigate the situation. I notice a car flipped over, completely upside down. I think, *please let everyone be all right.* The young driver and companion made it out of the car, I see. I assumed they slid out of the windows. I didn't ask. Instead I shouted, "Should I call 911?" not knowing if that had been done by the two others who were witness to the crash. Long story short, first-responders arrived and everything was dealt with. I was amazed at how, once again, life and death were in my face.

About three weeks after the diagnosis, I had a phone consultation with a psychologist I had been working with for almost two years. Initially, I hired him as my therapist because I was working for an agency and in a field that left me with secondary traumatic stress and vicarious traumatization. In addition, I was completely identified with community-based non-profits and the trauma field. I believed that my ability to sit with profound states of human suffering and have positive impacts with clients in such underfunded workplaces would have little influence on my health or well-being. At this moment in time, this sounds laughable. After we worked on my own healing for many months, I resigned from the agency where I was employed. Furthermore, I committed to working for myself via private practice. From there, I continued to work with this psychologist but as a consultant in order to have an additional set of eyes and ears on my most challenging cases. This shift was and has been very helpful. Then, during that very phone consultation I mentioned above, I first asked a couple case-related clinical questions, then told him of my recent diagnosis. After I rambled on about it and my action plan for almost 30 minutes, he shared with me his surprise. He told me that he had recently been diagnosed with pancreatic cancer. Unfortunately, the details of his case were anything but ideal and it sounded like it was advanced. This was terribly sad. We both took deep breaths and shared some resources. We also scheduled our next phone meeting for four weeks out before ending the call. I was glad when we talked again a month later to learn that his treatments were ongoing. As the months passed and the lack of contact grew, I prayed for him. Not knowing is difficult. Later, I learned of his passing.

Throughout the day, and that entire season, actually, I continued to ask myself, "What am I supposed to be learning at this time in my life?" The quick answer is to not take anything or anyone for granted, but equally so, how to rely on myself for direction with regard to health and healing. I began to take personal responsibility to a whole new level.

Other crises also emerged through the fall and the winter of 2019–2020. The question *What does this all mean*? ran through my mind almost constantly. I learned of friends who survived car accidents. Others lost beloved pets. Another friend lost her sibling—a surprise death. Another had a child hospitalized. There was so much pain, devastation, and loss. COVID-19 erupted around the world bringing with it additional challenges, hardship and death. What was around the corner? Some days I was afraid to open my eyes to look.

What are we truly supposed to learn from our own life experiences like these or from the experiences of others? Beyond the preciousness of life, I certainly cannot tell you, but I can offer tools and methods that anyone can utilize to find that answer themselves. Each one of us is unique. If what mystics and spiritual healers tell us about the nature of existence, energy and the world is true, then we are all connected, we are all one. With this in mind, what one experiences, we all experience. We can make the conscious decision to heal an aspect of ourselves (whether we go on to physically live another year or not) and perhaps even bring healing to others and to the planet. In a way, this book, *Dream Medicine*, offers some ways to bring healing into the world, not just for the individual, but for all.

Introduction

DREAMING HAS BEEN MY GATEWAY for much renewal and healing in my life. We have been dreaming since the beginning of time. Societies and cultures worldwide have long held particular beliefs about this state of existence, often pointing to the sacred or spiritual. Over the past century, Western science has made great advancements in its attempts to understand the phenomena, relegating it to profane or secular domains. Rapid eye movement (REM) sleep, and its connection to dreaming, wasn't even scientifically discovered until the 1950s. A handful of valuable how-to and self-help books on dreaming came out in the 1970s. These books were helpful to those wanting to incorporate dreaming into their healing/health practices by showing how dreams might reflect waking life issues, assist one in overcoming fears or problems, and show how to ask dreams for help by way of dream incubation. In 1997, the book *An Introduction to the Psychology of Dreaming* by Kelly Bulkeley was published. Dream research and theory development about why people dream and the function of dreaming have come a long way since that time, yet today, there is not one single agreed-upon definition of dreaming. In *Why We Sleep: Unlocking the Power of Sleep and Dreams* (2017), Matthew Walker reports how dreams fuel unique artistic gifts and revelations and solve problems, continuing the current dialogue surrounding the value of dreaming.

Since the completion of my first book, *Extraordinary Dreams: Visions, Announcements and Premonitions Across Time and Place*, it's been a thrilling ride—a journey that continues to deepen, showing me more and more about what it means to be a healer, to be conscious, and to be a caring, compassionate human. The state where I reside refers to us as Licensed Professionals of the Healing Arts (LPHA). Yes, I hold a state license to practice psychotherapy in California. Much of what I have learned in regard to holistic intuitive healing was taught to me *outside* of getting my CEs—those are the units of continuing education mandated by the state. With a PhD in clinical somatic psychology and as a spiritually informed, holistic psychotherapist, I combine evidence-based treatment with soulful, embodied-living practices in order to assist others in their healing journeys. I have found relatively few CE opportunities for those in my profession that include training in energy systems of the human body, altered/nonordinary states of consciousness, dreaming, or even including the concept of the soul. The vast majority of people across the world share the belief in the existence of the soul, "of a life-bearer in the form of a consciousness only loosely associated with a body" (Kalweit, 1984, p. 21). Using what I've been taught from my certifications in hypnotherapy and a sleep-based mediation called yoga nidra, I know that alternative ways and intuitive development can compliment Western conventional treatments. Talk therapy and analytical thinking have their limitations. Some of my best decisions have been made because of vivid nocturnal dreams and some of my greatest hopes have emerged from trance-induced daydreams. Viewing the human body as a grouping of compartmentalized parts can only get us so far. We have so much available to us in support of health and healing, whether that is our breath, our story, our body, our conscious awareness, our energy systems, our personal myths, or our dreams.

On one important level, psychotherapy is about relationships. One way I check in with myself about the relationships I have with others in my life is through dreams. Some years back, I was in a new relationship in which I felt some concerns. I was definitely a bit uncertain. One memorable dream reflected what I likely already knew deep inside of myself but acted as a force for immediate change.

I'm in the passenger seat of his car. He is driving us somewhere—possibly to our new home. We are on the edge, between a tall cliff and the sea. His driving is somewhat erratic. It is unsafe and water is getting in the car. When we arrive to our destination, I notice that the house is at the edge of a cliff. Despite the beautiful view, the house is barren, lifeless, and rickety. I felt alone there.

After logging this dream into my dream journal, I reflected on it for a couple days. Long story short, that dream was my best helper. I soon ended the draining and disappointing relationship after the dream took place. It turned out to be a very good decision. Our nocturnal dreams can help us in many ways. Decision-making, self-healing, and getting to the heart of a matter are just some examples.

This book takes us on a winding path, even touching on some murky concepts, to places that have taught me so much about what it means to exist and what has made me the person I am today. This book is personal and it is for anyone, not just healing professionals, not just dreamers and visionaries. I share personal experiences, stories of healing practitioners from cultures or groups other than my own, some research, and even tidbits from my own studies and discoveries over the past decade and beyond. My hope is that anyone who reads this book comes away with increased trust in their inner knowing, a sense of magic and wonder, an expansive view on what is possible, in addition to some solid exercises, tools and practices to engage with regularly. Dreams/visions in support of health practices will be viewed through a wide angle lens in this book. Health and wellness maintenance can take place in any state of consciousness. Read on to find out how.

But first, during the writing of this introduction I got another surprise. I checked my email only to learn that one of the local neighborhood bears had been declared a nuisance to some people in the community, causing property damage, and so he was killed. A legal execution order was signed. I had delighted in the times that this bear would visit me, either passing through the front yard or exploring my back deck. It was there that I noticed that when he stood up, we were eye to eye. I'm often saddened that people move into the forest—we are in Northern California—yet become so bothered by those we share the forest with that decisions are made to eliminate them. Sure, it takes a great deal of adjustments and inconvenience to live alongside wild animals—that is true and it is not easy. Sometimes we humans lose out. Pets and other animals can become prey. My doors have double locks and my pantry food is kept sealed in glass jars. I do not cook meat, as plant foods and their scents are less attractive to most wild creatures. In addition, garbage is contained in a "bear bin" away from the house. Snacks are not left in my car. Even though this bear was my neighbor too, I was never consulted about whether he should live or die. I was upset about this. You may be wondering why I am so bothered that I would announce this in the introduction to my book. Well, you see, I came to regard this bear as a friend. Before I ever physically saw this bear I knew him from my dreams. In dreamland he was clever and playful and he made me laugh as he ran circles around my small house. I always woke up feeling great and positively charged. Bears are powerful in many ways, and powerful medicine among many traditional peoples. Some tell about how the Bear is healer. Bear medicine men are regarded by the Lakota as the most powerful of healers. Others claim that Bear is the keeper of the dreamtime, thus storing the dreams' big lessons until the dreamer wakes up to them. Cherokee healer Dr. Loretta Standley noted this on her website: Bear people are considered "dreamers" due to their ability to tap into their intuition during the meditative process, thereby visualizing and manifesting newness. Bear reminds you not to cast your dreams aside, but to pay attention to them.

The killing of this bear as I wrote this book did not go unnoticed. As I sit here now, I wonder what they did with his body. Was he honored in any way? Tonight, before bed, I will initiate the art of dream incubation (a practice I teach in this book), hoping to see my deceased bear neighbor or sense his presence and energy once more. There, in the dream space, I can offer Bear something that I cannot offer elsewhere. In the waking state, a small shrine will do.

With that said, while you and I are here, on this beautiful planet together, I hope to offer you something through these pages that I may not be able to offer elsewhere. *Dream Medicine* was written as a holistic and spiritually inspired guide for health and healing. I hope you enjoy what you find in the chapters ahead. May your dreams be your medicine.

ONE

Medicinal Dreaming

IN THIS CHAPTER, I'll offer broad definitions for the terms *dream* and *medicine*. In my life, many aspects of medicine as well as the dream arts are part of my spirituality. Spirituality "refers to an appreciation of intangible yet meaningful aspects of our lives. The intangibles may be values (love, truth, peace), God, a life force, interpersonal connections, or perhaps a sense of transcendence" (Germer, 2005, p. 23). There are many approaches to spirituality, spanning from the immanent (the divine presence being pervasive and inherent) to the transcendental (the experience of mystical experiences). Instead of contrasting these, I value all of the above, preferring to practice daily mindful living alongside set dedicated times when I make space for deeper meditative practices which have offered an experience of union with Source. After dedicating many years as a student to diverse approaches, both Eastern and Western, I can say that I have learned a lot and hold great respect for spiritual and energetic arts such as shamanic journeying, meditative chanting, and conscious dreaming as well as here-and-now, moment-to-moment mindful awareness. I honor and value it all. And through it all I have come to a personal understanding of life force—a doorway by which we can experience much more than meets the (physical) eye.

> "Dive into yourself and in your soul you will discover the stairs by which to ascend."—Isaac of Nineveh

Dreams Are Real Experiences

First and foremost, dreaming is a *real* experience. And we all dream. About five years of one's life are spent sleeping and dreaming.

Still, there is no universally agreed upon definition of a dream. This may sound surprising given that dreaming is such a hot topic these days (dreams made the cover of both *Scientific American* and *Psychology Today* recently) and that the first dream was recorded more than 4,000 years ago. This ancient Sumerian dream is found within the Epic of Gilgamesh and can be located on the first of twelve clay tablets.

> Gilgamesh got up and revealed the dream, saying to his mother:
> "Mother, I had a dream last night.
> Stars of the sky appeared,
> and some kind of meteorite of Anu fell next to me.
> I tried to lift it but it was too mighty for me,
> I tried to turn it over but I could not budge it.
> The Land of Uruk was standing around it,
> the whole land had assembled about it,
> the populace was thronging around it,
> the Men clustered about it,
> and kissed its feet as if it were a little baby.
> I loved it and embraced it as a wife.
> I laid it down at your feet,
> and you made it compete with me."

Most traditional societies agree that the dream world is connected with a spiritual realm or the gods—dreaming is a way to communicate with the divine. We might only recall fragments or snippets of these lived experiences, yet they can impact our physiology as well as mental and emotional states. How can any experience that alters physiological responses while at times also affecting how one feels not be considered a real experience?

But What Is a Dream?

A dream is typically thought of as a visual, auditory, emotional or tactile memory in one's mind during the sleep cycle. But dreaming doesn't begin or end there. Let's also add to this definition of dreaming views from other people and places across time: the images, sensations, and feelings one experiences while falling asleep or while waking up from sleep. These are known as the hypnopompic and hypnagogic states, respectively. They are important because many people report various phenomena during those times as well as an amazing ability to connect the dots when it comes to solving problems or gaining meaningful insights. But let us not stop there. How about stretching the boundaries a little to also include experiences from trance, meditative, and ecstatic states (those experienced during shamanic or imaginal journeying)? Brain waves slow down in general, while some specific brain regions become active in those nonordinary states. It can feel similar to falling asleep or waking up and at the same time there is a unique alertness. All of this can be considered "dreaming."

To stretch the boundaries even further, let's include all dream-like states, experiences of the *imaginal world*: a realm said to exist beyond the ordinary cosmos and conventional world. The imaginal can include varying nonordinary states such as hypnopompia, hypnagogia, journeying, deep relaxation, meditative states, and hypnosis—these are just some examples. With regard to definitions and purposes of dreaming, I will quote one of my teachers, Robert Moss: "We dream to wake up. Dreaming is not fundamentally about what happens during sleep. It is about waking up to a deeper order of reality. Dreaming is a discipline; to get really good at it requires practice, practice, practice" (2014, p. 12). Later in this book, ways to engage in such practices and develop our connection with the imaginal realm will be explored.

For some, dreams are simply the result of the brain's chemical and electrical impulses with little meaning (a view known as the activation synthesis hypothesis), while some posit that dreams reflect our waking life concerns (continuity hypothesis) and for others dreams are connected to divinity and the spirit world, prompting action. Views on dreaming are vast. Ancient Greeks, as one example, created depictions of Asclepius healing through dreams, while modern day Greek youth view these things as fantasy and myth. The views surrounding dreaming are vast and fall somewhere along a very wide spectrum, depending on the group or individual and the time and location.

For ages, dreaming has served people in many ways, most of which are unknown to the dreamer. The purposes range from memory consolidation, emotional downloading, threat simulation and other evolutionary functions to the psychological fulfillment of desires and wishes, compensating for what life lacks, and more. The dreaming mind even helps us professionally, via problem solving and creative inspiration. Regarding professional pursuits, psychologist Dr. Deirdre Barrett (2017) explains, "While Western mathematicians have occasionally made major breakthroughs in their dreams, India's greatest mathematician, Srinivasa Ramanujan, said that all his mathematical proofs came to him in dreams and that he attributed them to the goddess Namagiri, to whom he had been taught to pray for dreams" (p. 65). Garnering solutions to problems in dreams goes well beyond the lives of mathematicians. In her 2001 book *The Committee of Sleep*, Barrett describes the many creative ways other professionals have used their dreams for solving problems. Diverse groups, such as artists, scientists and athletes, share their experiences here. If you are searching for ways in which your dreams can serve you, look no further.

If you are thinking, why not with healing? Well, it has! Dreaming, and dream-like states, are avenues for becoming aware of unsuspected health issues, gaining insight into health-related matters, and even healing. Diagnosis and healing in dreams is nothing new. It is just not spoken of or written about nearly as much as other areas of dreaming in modern Western cultures. Ancient Western societies (as well as many other societies) did, in fact, record dreams as meaningful and important for prophecy, diagnostics, and healing. (Problem solving dreams among contemporary healing professions, such as those of today's medical doctors and nurses, will be explored later.) I'd like to explicitly point out, up front, that dream content has different meaning in differing religions and various cultural groups. Take native Amharic language speakers of Ethiopia's Amhara region, for example. This group believes that a dream in which one's front tooth is taken out or missing indicates the approaching death of a close relative or loved one (Kinfemichael & Raju, 2017). A dream of this sort will likely be interpreted differently in another region, nation or religious group. This should serve as a reminder that dream dictionaries are of little use. The dream belongs to the dreamer, meaning that the dreamer holds the ultimate authority on his or her dream meaning or significance. The above-mentioned group is tight-knit and shares deep cultural beliefs and behaviors; therefore, such an interpretation works for them and may not be well understood by outsiders. Another example could be a dream featuring a black cat as the central image. Some groups view black cats with suspicion, while others see them as adorable and just as wonderful as any color of feline. Time and place make the difference when it comes to response or reaction.

In addition to distinctions between time and place, religion and spiritual differences are well noted, as I touched on above. Let me drive the point home further by adding views on dreams and visions from major religious perspectives. In the contemporary, traditional and mystic writings of Judaism, Christianity, and Islam significant dreams can be found (Csordas, 1994; Fahd, 1966). In Judaism, the more one dreams, the more worthy that person is of divine inspiration (Covitz, 1990). In some Christian churches, the sharing of dreams has been a part of the service (Charsley, 1973). A rich and complex dream culture can be found in Islam where three types of dreams are distinguished: true dreams from God, dreams from the devil, and earthly spirit dreams from the body of the dreamer.

We All Need Medicine

Medicine aims to promote wellness—individual and community—and it is the field of health and healing. According to the *Merriam-Webster Dictionary*, medicine is a substance or preparation used in treating disease; the science and art dealing with the maintenance of health and the prevention, alleviation, or cure of disease; and the branch of medicine concerned with the nonsurgical treatment of disease. The same dictionary defines wellness as the quality or state of being in good health especially as an actively sought goal. Actively seeking wellness, or a quality/state of being in good health, is not exclusive to humans. Animals are known to self-medicate, using plants to alleviate aches, pains and a variety of conditions. For us humans, medicine, today, seems to be associated with a pill, curative liquid or procedure; however, medicine, in general, is *any health practice*. These practices can be in support of physical, emotional, mental and spiritual health. The National Wellness Institute acknowledges "wellness" as multi-dimensional, a continuum spanning multiple domains (emotional, occupational, physical, social, intellectual and spiritual). To be well is an active process pointing us in the direction of a successful existence. The National Wellness Institute's webpage *About Wellness* notes that wellness is a positive and an affirming as well as a conscious, self-directed and evolving process of achieving full potential. Dedicated to the advancement of holistic medicine, the Foundation for Living Medicine seeks to bridge the gap between holistic and allopathic medicine, embracing the whole person in the healing process, not just honing in on the symptoms or disease. The following paragraph is borrowed from their website, http://www.thefoundationforlivingmedicine. org.

> The term, "Living Medicine," is based on the ancient Native American definition of "MEDICINE," which means "LIFE." Therefore, the term, "Living Medicine," translates to "Living Life." It is the process of living one's life and following one's individual path to Wholeness. Specifically, our lives represent a journey that each of us is taking in order to be WHOLE—emotionally, physically, mentally, and spiritually. Living Medicine is the name of that journey. By consciously "Living" our lives and "Listening to the Physician Within," we are practicing the "Medicine" that we need for growing and healing physically, mentally, emotionally, and spiritually. Paramount to the Living Medicine approach is the fundamental ideal that Love and Life are the true healers. Living Medicine recognizes each individual as a WHOLE Spiritual Being who creates their own recipe for living life and who does best when following their own unique path. It empowers each individual to take charge of their own life by consciously working with the Physician Within.

The Foundation for Living Medicine empowers us to take responsibility for our health and calls attention to preventative measures. Considering these broad definitions, medicine and wellness may be thought of as both a scientific and creative action—the art or process of providing treatment or ritual as well as a noun, meaning a variety of concoctions to apply or ingest.

Is illness an unfortunate accident? An isolated event? Or could illness result from how the body expresses beliefs, patterns, or psycho-social concerns? Doctors disagree here. While views from Western societies appear to be expanding, it is not across the board:

> If we were able to understand sickness and suffering as processes of physical and psychic transformation ... we would gain a deeper and less biased view of psychosomatic and psychospiritual processes and begin to realize the many opportunities presented by suffering and the death of the ego. Our long continuous battle against death and sickness has so deeply taken root in our consciousness that even modern psychology has felt compelled to take up the cudgel against physical weakness and dying. Consequently, psychic and physical suffering have remained unacknowledged as a means of altering consciousness and as forces and mechanisms of transformation and self-healing [Kalweit, 1984, p. 75].

Conventionally trained medical doctor Lissa Rankin (2013) wrote about her perceptual shift in her book *Mind Over Medicine*. Once she had the opportunity to work in an integrative clinic where she got to spend an hour with each patient, she changed her intake questionnaire. From her experiences, her new intake form included questions well beyond the standard conventional ones. In addition to asking about past medical and family histories, surgeries, substance use, and general health (sleep, exercise, diet), she had the time to inquire deeply into the patients' lives. Rankin now asked about their relationships, creative pursuits, level of happiness and fulfillment, spiritual connections, deepest desires and current stressors too. She discovered that even those that appeared to be the epitome of good health could become very ill when interpersonal and intrapersonal aspects of their lives were not well or greatly out of balance. Rankin asked her patients directly, "What do you think might lie at the root of your illness?" and "What does your body need to heal?" (2013, p. 69). To her surprise, many of her patients expressed that they believed that the root cause of their illnesses and the healing remedy may be related to factors in their day-to-day lives, such as unhappy marriages, loneliness, avoidance, forgiveness, or being out of alignment with life purpose and greater truths.

This is where dream medicine comes into play. Our dreams and visionary states can mirror back to us root causes, what may be suppressed or completely missing from our lives and what we need most to thrive. They can show us how connected we truly are to spirit, nature, and life unfolding all around us. For many, these experiences offer profound spiritual connection. No matter where we sit along the continuum, we can use nonordinary states as vehicles for personal growth, wellness, and self-transformation. We may even feel a deep sense of spiritual support prompting us to take direct action steps toward wholeness and optimal health.

In addition, how one "gets well" is as wide as the heavens. Time, place and culture all come into play. Some cultures claim that in order to heal, the soul body must be in balance, congruent, because the soul body is where the causes of illnesses reside (Kalweit, 1984). Healers, shamans and medicine people act in any state of consciousness, whether that is a waking, trance, or dream state, and may give one or more remedies from nature in any or all of these states. By doing so, attention to disease (dis-ease) prevention, alleviation, or cure takes place anywhere, anytime. This is also the case for receiving guidance or assistance regarding which methods or remedies are likely to be most effective. Providing treatment can be equally effective in any or all states of awareness. For instance, a patient may come to the home of a healer, share a meal, and report symptoms, yet receive the healing treatment in the dream state at a later time. In other cases, a patient may drive to a medical center, enter an office and interact with a person in a white coat, then 15–20 minutes later leave the building with a little piece of paper (a prescription) without the need to return to that particular treatment provider ever again. These interactive, prescriptive, and relationship differences will depend on the culture. In this book, we will explore health-related practices that have been inspired and shaped by dreams and visions and meditative spaces as well as dream states that have prompted healing in some way because dreaming (in all its related manifestations) is medicinal.

There is more to life than the material world. Side note: We can connect with the divine in many ways, without ever consuming psychedelics (hallucinogenic substances). Why do I name psychedelics specifically? I do so because when I speak of dream medicine, some have inquired about them. I'm not saying that psychedelics, as an appropriately utilized tool, are bad or not worthy of attention. Instead, I'm saying that we can have our most profound questions answered, feel deeply connected to Source and our higher self, and gain inner knowledge and more through practicing techniques and strategies that elevate consciousness without ingesting any substances at all. Many of the practices described in this book do not deliver instant enlightenment, however, through ongoing commitment, this *slower road* just might lead to a deeper integration and to long-lasting transformation.

From 2018 through 2020, I spoke with two authors that intend to bring dreaming back into Western medicine: holistic radiologist Larry Burk, MD, Duke University Medical School, and three-time breast cancer survivor Kathleen O'Keefe-Kanavos. Their 2018 book is titled *Dreams That Can Save Your Life: Early Warning Signs of Cancer and Other Diseases.* Burk and O'Keefe Kanavos both had dreams warning of breast cancer either for themselves or for close friends. Conventional Western medicine is not very friendly toward the use of dreams as diagnostic tools, yet the countless reports of how they have saved lives warrants taking a more open-minded approach. One example was when Burk's 2016 TEDx talk in Raleigh, North Carolina, was censored or banned due to claims that it was unscientific. Cancer-focused radiologists, like Burk, need to think outside of the box and be open-minded, in my opinion. After all, we haven't cured cancer yet. The TEDx coaches encouraged Burk to be very conservative and to approach everyone in the audience as a skeptic. They even encouraged him to wear a suit instead of the shirt he had chosen. Burk shared with me how he complied with the demands and approached his presentation conservatively. You can find his TedX talk on YouTube today with this link: www.youtube.com/watch?v=q_sQIQvwCII. I hope you watch it and see for yourself. We believe it is important for all meaningful patient experiences to be heard, believed, and considered when it comes to health and healing options. Burk and I both watched Dr. Christopher Kerr's Tedx Buffalo talk "I See Dead People," available on YouTube. In his talk, Kerr focused on dreams of the dying in palliative care. Some areas of medicine do appear to be a bit more open-minded.

Kathleen O'Keefe-Kanavos has survived breast cancer multiple times. Even when her doctors couldn't locate the cancer in her body or missed it altogether, her dreams revealed this frightening diagnosis. Her dreams also gave detailed information as to the location of the cancer. She shares the story of how, even after three healthy blood tests, mammogram reports, and physical exams, recurring dreams would send her back to her doctor's office. In one dream, a monk showed her the exact spot where the cancer was growing and recommended she fight to be granted exploratory surgery. Turns out, the dream was correct. Surgery revealed a tumor, and pathologists discovered cancer hiding inside that tumor. Kathleen survived. This experience, however, was only the first. To go the distance and travel the rest of her journey, refer to *Dreams That Can Save Your Life: Early Warning Signs of Cancer and Other Diseases.*

Dreams and visions can be a part of any health-related practice. They can provide us with valuable diagnostic information, alerting us to developing health issues in the body long before symptoms are detected. This would be what is known as precognitive dreaming, which is when a dream provides foreknowledge of an event. This is also known as a premonition. Carl Jung may have provided an explanation for this phenomenon in his book *Man and His Symbols.* He wrote: "Thus, dreams may sometimes announce certain situations long before they actually happen. This is not necessarily a miracle or form of precognition. Many crises in our lives have a long unconscious history. We move toward them step-by-step, unaware of the dangers that are accumulating. But what we consciously fail to see is frequently perceived by our unconscious, which can pass the information on through our dreams" (1964, p. 36).

I'll share one of my dreams from March 2019—it came just over six months prior to my medical diagnosis. Could this dream have been precognitive? Could my body have been trying to deliver an important message that I would consciously register?

I'm with a group of female friends. One of them does something that feels divinatory—a charting of some kind. It's circular and reflects various symbols, images and words. I don't recognize it, but it is something related to my health. They give me directions and instructions for something I need to do for my health. Do I need a special practitioner? Is it something huge? I need to figure out what my body needs.... I'm assured that this issue isn't huge or life-threatening, but it is a message to attend to my body and psyche and to give it what it needs. I need to make adjustments, take certain vitamins or something but I don't recall exactly.

In addition to showing the dreamer what is to come, dreams can even show us diverse avenues for healing. Pay attention in all states of consciousness, for you might discover the unexpected. One woman, in her late thirties at the time, dreamed of a home intruder who aimed a gun at her breast. She believed this to be a warning so she sought medical attention. This revealed early-stage cancer; she and her medical provider took action. After a lumpectomy, the health problem was resolved (Moss, 2005).

Dreams can have a lasting impact on the dreamer's health. Dreams may be healing, and conscious dreamers may use dreams as part of a fulfilling wellness practice, and at the same time, dreams can be tormenting, causing some to lose sleep and even negatively impacting one's nervous system. Take trauma, for instance. Recurring disturbing dreams are one element that may arise from traumatic stress. The current edition of the *Diagnostic and Statistical Manual of Mental Disorders* (DSM 5) includes post-traumatic stress disorder (PTSD). One criterion of PTSD is recurrent distressing dreams in which the content and/or effect of the dream is related to the traumatic experience. For children, frightening dreams may arise without any recognizable content. (Later, sleep hygiene and other healthy behaviors that support experiencing peaceful slumber will be discussed.)

Now, I will give attention to a common yet often misunderstood concept: the dreamcatcher. A few years ago, I worked with two Native American clients who were from opposite ends of the United

States and Canada—both were young mothers who attended individual and group trauma therapy sessions every week. They shared with the group members different beliefs and traditions related to dreams and dreaming. One of the women identified herself as Navajo and the other as Cayuga with Ojibwa children. The Cayuga mother taught the group about what a dreamcatcher actually is and its function, as it is an Ojibwa tradition. Dreamcatchers are meant to support children's health and well-being by catching bad dreams while allowing the favorable dreams to pass through. She also explained misconceptions and how to handle the dreamcatcher properly before leading the group in making one. She and I collected some of the necessary supplies from nature during the following month. Then, she led each participant in creating a dreamcatcher to take home. We used thin, flexible branches to craft a hoop and synthetic sinew to hold it together. No knots or glue were to be used. Next, the complex "web" pattern was designed to allow a small hole in the center, then one "spider" was added—a bead made of wood or bone. The final instruction included adding a few feathers to fall below, hanging from the hoop. Over the years, several feathers have been given to me either as a kind gesture or a thank you gift. I chose a hawk, a turkey, and a third unidentified gifted feather to hang from my dreamcatcher. While our Cayuga instructor told us that these are meant to be hung above children's beds to protect them, it was appropriate for us adult women to use them ourselves. Everyone was happy to participate in the activity and learn. The Cayuga woman also expressed the importance of the dreamcatcher getting touched by sun's morning rays, therefore, we were to hang these in specific locations in specific ways. As the group session came to a close, I noticed the pleasant energy in the room. Everyone was content. We had come together in a traditional ritual rooted in community, health, and dreaming.

Two

Consciousness and Shamanism

CONSCIOUSNESS IS A TERM used in a variety of ways with dozens of definitions. Krippner describes consciousness as "the pattern of an organism's perceptual, cognitive, and affective activities and/or experiences at any given moment in time. An alteration of consciousness is a significant shift or deviation in an organism's customary pattern as experienced by that organism and/or observed by others" (2000, p. 101). An altered state is associated with shamanic experiences. These nonordinary states can come about by various means—drumming, visualizing, fasting, concentrating, running, chanting, sensory deprivation, dancing, lucid dreaming, and silence are some examples. Such technologies are employed by shamans to achieve special conscious states, and typically two or more are used together. Krippner goes on to remind his readers that the distinction of conscious states, between ordinary and nonordinary, is socially and culturally dependent. This is an important point.

So let's go a little deeper and investigate humankind's first mystical tradition, the most ancient of all medical, religious and psychological disciplines, known today as shamanism. The word shaman originated from the language of the Tungus people of Siberia (Harner, 1990). According to several experts and scholars on the topic, shamanism may be considered a "spiritual belief and a practice of psychological consciousness" (Lee & Kanazawa, 2015, p. 265). We can think of it as "the earliest spiritual practice known to humankind, dating back tens of thousands of years" (Ingerman, 2004/2008, p. 7), emerging from every continent of the world across time. Shamanism is a complex phenomenon and "coexists with other forms of magic and religion"—it is a "technique of ecstasy" (special types of dreams and trance states) along with "mastery of fire" and "magical flight" (Eliade, 2004, pp. 4–5) and so much more, as we will see. Anthropologists, psychologists, and other scholars have used the term *shaman* to describe non–Western people who may have previously been called several unrelated (and sometimes even pejorative) terms such as seer, magician, wizard, sorcerer, witch, medicine man, or witch doctor. These terms are not exactly interchangeable, and many of those who identify with the above terms are not shamans. The shaman can be any of the above. Another way to view this is to consider shamanism as a "group of techniques by which practitioners enter the 'spirit world,' purportedly obtaining information that is used to help and heal members of their social group" (Krippner, 2000, p. 93). Now used worldwide, strictly speaking, the term shaman references a phenomenon originating from Siberia and central Asia (Krippner, 1994).

Romanian religious historian and professor Mircea Eliade (1907–1986) made a most significant mark on the study of shamanism with his seminal 1951 publication *Shamanism: Archaic Techniques of Ecstasy*, which offers an in-depth (yet somewhat problematic) look at the world of shamanism, focusing on shamans of central and northeast Asia. Today, Eliade's book is both a necessary read and a controversial one in the world of scholars of shamanism.

Shamans are particular types of healers who serve their communities. Helping people in their communities is key. Mastering the art of escaping the mind-body complex is crucial so that journeying and shapeshifting and entering other realms of existence can occur (Cowan, 1993). The shaman's soul leaves the body, traveling to the sky or lower world, through a special form of trance, and the shaman also has control in communication with spirits "without thereby becoming their instrument" (Eliade, 2004, p. 6). These conditions are distinct from those of mediumship, for shamans maintain attentional control and awareness, unlike a medium. This distinction is an interesting one. While both medium and shaman engage in altered states of consciousness, it is "the shaman's attention, memory, and awareness [that] seem to be enhanced, not restricted" (Krippner, 2000, p.

153). Furthermore, shamans have been *elected*, thereby given access to spiritual manifestations and the ability to effectively work with them, whereas for other community members, such sacred space is inaccessible (Eliade, 2004). While the body and mind adjusted through suffering serious, long-term psychic or physical illnesses, many shamans accessed "an alternate mode of perception" (Kalwet, 1984, p. 96). In many regions of the world, the shamanic profession is hereditary, passed down through family lines. Still, the proof is in the pudding, as they say—effectiveness in the healing work determines whether one holds onto the status of shaman.

Initiations

One can be called to follow many paths or to become many things. After the call to shamanize, which can be spontaneous, comes training and preparation, thereby moving one toward initiation. Initiation involves a ritual of some kind, and there are usually many of them, each one following a preparatory stage (Krippner, 1994). Sometimes, one is not aware of the call or that her body is undergoing an initiation process. This can be the case with illness. According to German ethnopsychologist Holger Kalweit, "The sicknesses that arise as a result of a calling are surely the highest form of illness—a sacred illness which by its power makes it possible for mystical and metaphysical insights to arise ... this frequently happens without regard to the feelings and wishes of the chosen one who, in most cases, is not aware of the fact that his body is undergoing an initiation" (1984, p. 89).

Initiation sites and methods differ—from waking state experiences to dreams—although the most stunning initiation is by lightning. Surviving a strike and emerging with supernatural abilities can directly shove someone onto the shamanic path. Lightning is, and has been, associated with power, and even holiness, through time and across great geographical distance, such as ancient Greece, Mongolia, throughout North and South America, northeast Africa, and well beyond (Kalweit, 1992). During the time I was writing my first book, *Extraordinary Dreams*, I became acquainted with an anthropologist from Spain, who at the time was visiting California. She spent much of her career going back and forth between her native Spain and South America where she lived with the Quechua of the Peruvian Andes. As our friendship developed, I went to visit her and her family at their home in Madrid. We spoke about her work and she told me about the importance of lightning. If one survives a lightning strike without dying, this event is likely to begin the initiatory process of ritual specialist for that community member (for full report see Mascaro, 2018).

Another initiation method is through dreams in which the future shaman sees himself or herself dismembered, cut into pieces, or tortured in some way by wild creatures, demons, ghosts, or other spirit beings. These intense and profound initiations result in transcending the human condition. Not all initiations, or even initial calls, to shamanism are as intense. For some tribes, it is dreaming vividly, dreaming of deceased relatives, or dreaming about the spirit world—even out-of-body activity. Essentially, dreaming carries a central role in shamanism (Laughlin & Rock, 2014). Age is not necessarily a factor as "future shamans can be selected at as early as nine years of age on the basis of their dreams" (Jones & Krippner, 2012, p. 116). The sex of the future shaman is not a factor either. Here is an example of an initiation process from the Paviotso, an American Plateau Shoshonean tribe living in Nevada: "A man dreams that a deer, eagle, or bear comes after him. The animal tells him that he is to be a doctor. The first time a man dreams this way he does not believe it. Then he dreams that way some more and he gets the things the spirit [ancestor] told him to get.... Then he learns to be a doctor. He learns his songs when the spirit comes and sings to him" (Park, 1934, p. 99).

Initiation sites vary greatly. Some appear to be more formal than others. In western Europe, "over 200 caves have been discovered ... elaborately designed with Paleolithic drawing of animals, shamans, handprints, and other esoteric symbols" (Cowan, 1993, p. 123). Scholars note the practice of sleeping in sites such as sacred underground sarcophagi among Irish pilgrims of the early Christian era, perhaps as a way to re-experience death and rebirth on the shamanic path (Cowan, 1993). Death and resurrection are an indication of initiation, which destroys and erases the former life, thus denoting entry to a new life phase—this is universal, having occurred over millennia across cultures and locations (Kalweit, 1984).

Tasks, Roles and Duties

Two of the many important tasks for many shamans are escorting the dying through the transition to death, into the otherworld, and helping to ensure abundance for the community, specifically with regard to the hunt (survival). First, I will touch on the dying process, as classic shamanic training that includes what we can consider death counseling or mediation. One aspect of this type of counseling is taking on the role of soul guide or psychopomp, one who leads the soul of a dying person into the next realm. Kalweit stated, "The shaman is the classic investigator of the realm of death; he explores the routes of travel to and in the Beyond and thereby produces a map of the postmortem terrain" (1984, p. 11). An additional duty of the psychopomp would be to journey to the spirit world to petition favor or obtain instruction from deities. Poetic speech, songs (especially those in particular frequencies), and magical words are part of the psychopomp's toolkit. Cowan (1993) would add trickery to this toolkit since, sometimes, a soul must be tricked into leaving this realm and heading toward the land of the dead.

I will share a vague, generalized version of a 2018 dream I can never forget, as it is too personal to convey in detail.

I am walking between two realms, the one of the living and a spirit realm. In the realm of the living, I witness family members caressing and supporting another family member in the dying process. Upon witnessing this, I then turn to my right and walk through a threshold or special doorway—like a portal. There, I speak with the spirit of the dying one. I share my gratitude, appreciation and love. I am given specific information and instruction, which I take with me as I pass through the threshold once again, to deliver to the living members of the family. I go through this back and forth process several times in this one dream—crossing from the world of the living to the other side and back again. I am there to serve a purpose, to play a role.

I do not appoint myself to such a role, psychopomp or otherwise, although I shared this unforgettable dream with you here; an impactful experience arose spontaneously. Having had many dreams of the deceased, from acquaintances to friends and family members, I can tell you that this particular dream was extraordinarily different. What does it mean?

As for community abundance, shamans provide assistance to hunters in locating game animals. The relations are spiritual in their very nature. Shamans dream or journey to the wild animal's location. As the animal reveals itself to the shaman, and the fertile area is located, hunters go out to harvest such resources for the community. Eliade (2004) adds, "donning the skin of an animal was becoming the animal, feeling himself transformed into the animal. We have seen that, even today, shamans believe that they can change themselves into animals" (p. 459). See Eliade's chapter 12 for ancient Chinese "bear ceremonialism." The hunter (shaman, in this sense) and the hunted must become one, moving physically and psychically between worlds (Cowan, 1993). This shapeshifting transformation of becoming the animal ensures the greatest possible success.

A while after Eliade, anthropologist Michael Harner (1929–2018) conducted prolonged fieldwork in a different region of the world. He lived with the Jivaro of the Ecuadorian Andes and the Conibo of the Peruvian Amazon, learning much from both groups over time. All this took place between 1956 and 1973. From all he had absorbed, Harner created what he called *core shamanism* to encompass the near-universal principles, common features, and practices of shamanism not bound to any specific cultural group or perspective. Core shamanism includes journeys to other worlds, as this is a distinguishing feature of shamanism, through one of the many brain wave shifting sonic driving methods.

Drumming is one such method. Wall paintings from ancient Turkey (5600 BCE) feature drums. Various constructions of drums are used in numerous cultures across all inhabited continents, going by diverse terms such as the shaman's horse, the whip, or the rainbow bridge (Jones & Krippner, 2012). Regardless of instrument, cosmic travel or soul flight (sometimes called an out-of-body experience by Western psychologists) is central regarding the shamanic journey, setting apart shamans from other ecstatics, healers, and mystics (Walsh, 1990, 2014). Natural features symbolize the cosmos allowing interaction with other realms—many landscapes exist for a shaman, not just one (Knight, 2015).

University of California professor of psychiatry, philosophy, and anthropology Roger Walsh (2014) poses a compressed definition: "Shamanism can be defined as a family of traditions whose practitioners focus on voluntarily entering altered states of consciousness in which they experience themselves or their spirit(s) interacting with other entities, often by traveling to other realms, in order to serve their community" (p. 15–16). This offers clarity so that the experience, practice, or method is not confused with a specific religion, dogma, faith, or belief; rather, shamanism is a spiritual, healing or consciousness discipline.

Even for geographically distant locations and distinct cultures, shamanic methods are similar (Harner, 1990). Because of religious oppression, Westerners lost almost all shamanic knowledge centuries ago. Shamanism in western Europe, however, can be traced as far back as 20,000 years ago. This knowledge goes back to the Stone Age, preceding "the Bible, Buddha, and Lao Tzu by tens of thousands of years" (Walsh, 1990, p. 3). It continues to live deep within human consciousness. According to Davidson (1981), "There are parallels in descriptions of shamanic ceremonies in northern Europe and Siberia" (p. 130). Getting help from spirit animals, hanging from trees, and using the shaman's "horse" are some examples of such parallels (Eliade, 2004). Another example could be attracting the shaman's spirit back into the body through special songs sung by young Sami (aka Lapp) women. After such rituals, the seeress (or any woman practicing divination in this way), would provide instruction or information regarding the future. These accessed trance states appear to be a common element regarding prophecy, however, the purpose and way through which one enters a state of ecstasy differ from group to group and place to place. Other ceremonies, involving sacrifice, share similar characteristics among ancient Greek, Siberian, and Arctic peoples (Eliade, 2004).

For those not born into shamanism or for those not elected at a young age, the call to shamanize, by way of dream or waking vision, may come as a surprise. Rejecting a call to shamanize is not a good idea, no matter the location or time. The price one may pay for such a rejection could range from misfortune to death. If spirit comes to your door, you must answer it.

One does not need to be a shaman to enter the imaginal realm just as anyone who is familiar with the imaginal realm is not a shaman. Sometimes the terms are intertwined together in books, presentations and workshops, however, I believe it is best to understand the distinctions as well as have an understanding where the two converge. Working in nonordinary states is nothing new or unique and has taken place across all of the world's cultures throughout time—shamanism is universal—yet Harner asks that the term shaman be reserved for indigenous shamanic healers, whereas non-indigenous healers are called shamanic practitioners.

I was privileged to host the Shift Network's 2020 Dreamwork Summit. Sandra Ingerman, a teacher of shamanic practices and shamanic journeying for over 40 years, was one of the guests I interviewed. She shared how shamanic work is similar to dreamwork and ways that dreamwork can manifest in shamanic practices. Sandra explained how nighttime dreams supported daily survival of communities, such as revealing the location of game for a successful hunt or warning of a danger to come. Dreams reflect our inner and outer worlds—the deepest part of our psyche or consciousness. Sandra continued to speak about daytime dreams, another type of dreaming practice. In our daytime dreams, "we are making everything up"—we make up who we see, the conversation, "the landscape we are in, so in shamanic cultures it is believed that we are dreaming the wrong dream," she explained. Our daydreams are reflecting our current experience: we are "dreaming the wrong dream"—and it's not looking so good, especially from an environmental point of view. Sandra taught us the "third type of dreaming practice in shamanism is shamanic journeys," which combines night and daydreams. In journeys we can't make up who comes to us and what they share (spirit guides, for example). We have control of our actions in shamanic journeys but not who reveals themselves to us. This is different from non-lucid dreams where we typically just go along with what is unfolding and different from daydreams where we have great control. Shamanic journeying is a bit of both, like a middle place, where we can control what we do or whether we choose to accept the guidance offered to us, but not necessarily what takes place in the spiritual worlds around us during those journeys.

I have experienced spontaneous nocturnal *lucid* dreams and have nonspontaneously or consciously induced a shamanic journey in the same day, so from personal experience, I can sense how these two states are distinct even though there is an element of personal control in both states. We will return to lucid dreaming later in this book. It is wise to remember that conventional treatments, both medical and psychological, can coexist alongside spiritual healings, such as those emerging from shamanism. In some cultures, physicians work alongside shamanic healers. There is no need to be in conflict when it comes to these treatments. Ingerman (2004/2008) shares the story of Connie (a pseudonym), who combined allopathic medical care with dreamwork and shamanic practice: "Connie was diagnosed with breast cancer. She chose to have a lumpectomy and radiation, as advised by her doctors. Combined with her traditional medical treatment, she journeyed to hummingbird and asked for help. She combined her shamanic work with dreamwork. Hummingbird instructed Connie to make breast casts and paint them with healing images. And then within a week she was given a grant to teach workshops on this healing method to women diagnosed with breast cancer" (p. 75). Good medicine comes in many forms. It can be full of pleasant surprises. Expect the unexpected.

In early 2021, I interviewed Lena Swanson about her experience with shamanic practices. She trained in core shamanism under Michael Harner for several years as well as with Sandra Ingerman. First, Swanson shared with me her call to the shamanic path. She had two different recurring dreams most of her life. These began in childhood, when she was very young. In one of these recurring dreams she was pursued in order to be persecuted and killed. It was terrifying, she said. The second recurring dream was nice and sweet. Swanson would dream of being in an old house. The house belonged to her and she was alone in it, although comfortable. She recalls, "I would open a door and find an entire part of the house, a really cool part of the house, I never knew existed." It would be filled with woodwork and old, beautiful things. Once she embarked on the shamanic path, both of these recurring dreams stopped.

After training with Ingerman, Swanson began offering healing services to others. I asked her how shamanic journeying can help a person to heal and whether she had worked with anyone who reported profound healing as a result. She told me that one of her clients who initially hired her for her animal communication services later requested a soul retrieval. She said that there was a delay in getting together for the session. After some time, when this client arrived to her appointment, she couldn't speak—"completely lost her voice" due to an emergency tracheotomy. The doctors told her that her voice would eventually come back, yet even after significant time passed, she could only whisper. This surprised the doctors. At the appointment, Swanson had difficulty hearing this client's voice: "I could barely understand her." Yet she proceeded as planned, conducting a shamanic soul retrieval session in her usual fashion, just as this client requested. Between that session and reconnecting with this client, a couple of months had passed. When this client called Swanson, her voice was back. Swanson was stunned! The client reported that her voice returned the very next day, following the soul retrieval session. She told Swanson that as she awoke from sleep the next morning, she found herself singing the same song Swanson had sung during the session, one she had never heard before that day. Miraculously, her voice was back! Listening to this story, I was taken aback by how it was the healing song that turned out to be the first "normal" sound emerging from this client's lips or, rather, vocal cords. Her voice could have returned any time and her first words could have been anything, however, the timing and vocalization, for me, are beyond coincidence. Swanson reflected on how spiritual healing can take place instantly, but the way this healing eventually manifests in the physical body can take time. Swanson advises her clients to slow down and allow time for the healing to integrate. Spirit works in mysterious ways. Always be on the lookout for synchronicity. Swanson also shared with me a memory of doing shamanic healing work on behalf of another client who had been disturbed by cluttering behavior for about 20 years, the home filled with needless items. After one session, the client returned home and completely removed these items, decluttering the home completely that same week. The shamanic healing session appeared to have supported the client in purging 20 years' worth of needless objects.

After sharing with Swanson my own history of entry into this work, I asked about her understanding of the similarities and differences with visions, dreams, and journeys. She described the way she practices having been trained in core shamanism. This way of journeying is "very intentional. State an intention for the journey, decide which world you will travel to (lower, middle or upper), plan to meet with your power animal or a teacher (and maybe go on a tour). Use the repetitive beat to go on the journey." These journeys are purposeful and clear, conducted with intentionality. Today, Swanson does not often recall her dreams, especially not since the years of recurring dreams came to an end. Within the last few months, however, Swanson's old house dreams have come back. She takes this to mean that a new part of her life, during this period, needs to be explored. Messages in shamanic journeys, just like dreams, can be metaphorical. One purpose for a shamanic journey could be to use that state to reenter a dream or continue the dream in order to gain additional information and broader understanding. "Simply set an intention to gain more clarity," Swanson said.

I asked Swanson about ancestral connections from a shamanic perspective. Sometimes one can exhaust all avenues for healing an issue without any positive progress. Swanson's primary experience with this has revolved around curses that "have been handed down, handed down and handed down. Each generation goes through the same stuff no matter what anyone does." ("It's like having a bleed through from a past life to this lifetime," she added.) If the curse is not unraveled in a particular generation, the same frequency, the same vibration comes through in each passing generation, she explains. Healing is important.

Connection with and service to our ancestors can be both beautiful and meaningful as well. Anthropologist Hank Wesselman participated in the Shift Network's 2020 Ancestral Healing Summit. During his interview, Wesselman spoke of the link between shamanism and ancestral ties. Using examples from his own life and the lives of his students, he dissected the processes involved with disease manifestation, such as throat cancer and breast cancer. He noted how a "distortion in the ancestral field" can be passed along generationally and can also be healed. This healing takes place through our own physical body, especially the heart center. The physical body is the barometer allowing one to connect with an ancestor and heal anything that has been passed along by that ancestor. This is all part of shamanic work. Skilled shamans can do this work for others, on their behalf. While connecting to multiple generations of ancestors is a common practice among various cultures and peoples of the world, it's best if those connections remain healthy ones.

THREE

Oracles, Divination
and Dream Medicine
in the Classical, Celtic, Nordic
and Germanic Worlds

COMMUNICATION BETWEEN HUMANKIND and the supernatural world is seeped in ancient tradition and ritual across the entire world, as we have seen. Oracles, whose tasks revolved around providing guidance, were honored in ancient times. Accessing hidden knowledge and participating in a continual communicative cycle with the unseen appears to be regaining popularity today. Oracles, divination and dreaming have dramatically entered contemporary Western language and behavior, but let us peek into the past, shall we?

Greco-Roman

In the book *Divination and Oracles*, Morrison (1981) writes, "Greeks always believed that the soul, or part of the soul, was somehow freed from inhibition of the body during sleep and could indicate truth of the present, past or, particularly, future, by means of dreams" (p. 109). Over the centuries, just how dreams were to be interpreted was not as straightforward. The Classical world is comprised of the Mediterranean regions spanning about 1,000 years, beginning in the 700s BCE. In its early period, oracles, dream interpretation, and divination were commonplace and can be found in Greek documents. In addition to the assigned expert practitioners, birds, snakes, fire, laurel, and oak trees, for example, played their part. Even necromancy (consulting the spirits of the deceased) and sacrifice were practiced. From all of this, prophecies, or predictions about the future, unfolded. These consultations were serious business, and fee for service was expected, whether for yes or no predictions or inspired responses or utterances. Oracle experts, priests or priestesses, prophets, and the like held respectable positions in society, therefore occupying important semi-official roles. While not as famous as Delphi, the first prophetic center was most likely the oracle at Dodona, dedicated to Zeus and the mother of Aphrodite, Dione.

As for the Delphic Oracle, dedicated to the god Apollo, it is believed that these practices continued for over a thousand years. Women were central here, as the Pythia of the time was considered the human vehicle for Apollo, his will passing through her as she remained in trance. Those consulting the Pythia were instructed to keep their minds clear and pure, as the Pythia may be under Apollo's influence at that very moment.

In school, ancient Romans learned to distinguish between two categories of omens—those given and those provoked. These practices are believed to have originated from the Etruscans, the indigenous peoples of central Italy that came from that area prior to the Roman civilization. We can take an example of a provoked omen from the time of the first Punic War: chickens refusing to eat when fed was considered unfavorable (Morrison, 1981). This is not a good sign when this form of divination is used to learn whether you will win a war.

Several decades later, Cicero, who once held the office of augur, wrote about divination. While it is still practiced, the deeper beliefs underneath seemed to have been waning. Most of the old philosophers, including Plato and Aristotle, believed in divination. Natural forms of divination, such as by dreams (oneiromancy), for example, were considered to hold the most power (Morrison, 1981). During the time of the Roman Empire, "divination was still practised by the college of augurs, but the ... growing influence of Christianity hastened the decline in belief in its truth" (p. 89).

That growing religious influence played a part in how the arts of divination were to develop. In addition, it would also determine how, and by whom, dreams were to be interpreted, whether regarding the past, revelations about the truth of a current situation, or even the future.

Diagnosing in the Dream State

The second century physician and philosopher Galen is considered the most important physician of the ancient world after Hippocrates. Galen published considerable amounts of work—his theories dominated European medicine for 1,500 years. Galen valued dreams personally and professionally. In Galen's treatise *On Diagnosis from Dreams,* dreams are presented as a medical diagnostic aid. However, it should not be assumed that this was Galen's primary diagnostic method. Galen suggested taking into account the dreamer's circumstances to determine the meaning of a dream. Galen also explained that the soul generates dreams that reflect the body's needs and overall condition, but he made it clear that not all dreams are medical ones (Hulskamp, 2013).

Today, it is nearly impossible to locate a contemporary medical journal containing an article highlighting medical diagnostics and dreams, although some physicians have told me that they believe dreams can point to a brewing illness or developing disease. This has been the case with cancer, among other diseases. The topic of dream diagnosis will resurface throughout this book.

Nordic, Germanic, Celtic

Pre-Christian Scandinavian, Nordic, Germanic, and Celtic peoples relied heavily on divination and auguries. Contained within first-century CE Latin writings, it was noted that Germans considered divination valuable for decision-making surrounding the life of family and tribe (Davidson, 1981). Even long after Christianization, runes continued to be used among Germanic and Scandinavian peoples. In addition to those more complex systems, simpler systems were used, such as systems that reveal a yes or no answer to a question posed by the querent. These forms of divination could be used for day-to-day matters or situations surrounding life or death such as sacrifices. When it came to decisions surrounding battle, Germans trusted the divinatory abilities of the older women. The outcome was taken very seriously.

A Germanic official divination system was horse or bird augury, but not just any horse or bird. It must be a white horse sacred to the gods or birds of the god Odin. For Nordic peoples, ravens in particular held a high status. Horse augury in other nearby regions may use a different color horse for such practices. In addition, the specific protocol for how the horse would be used differed depending on the area or group.

A female seer, or seeress, was often consulted by German tribespeople, as she was believed to hold prophetic powers and holy elements (Davidson, 1981). Official policy and other decisions were made after consultation with these women of prophecy. Similar to ancient Greek oracular tradition, these women also sat on a type of seat higher above ground than was typical.

With regard to dreaming, Icelandic literature suggests that dreams can be induced at will and reveals ways to restore dreams to those who do not recall them. Behaviors and practices for communicating with the gods, communicating with the dead, gaining information and inspiration, and even curing are noted (Davidson, 1981). Much of this became unlawful with the rise of Christianity, especially rituals involving communing with the deceased.

For some, even in today's modern times, "the ability to 'dream true' is still taken very seriously" (Davidson, 1981, p. 115) along with prophecy or revelation in Iceland and Northern Scandinavia.

Greece, Then and Now

From the legends of Asclepius to the writings of Xenophon, Greece is no stranger to dreams—this place held a most vibrant culture of dreaming. In June and July of 2019, I visited Greece to see with my own eyes evidence of a lost dream-focused culture. I spent time speaking with young Greeks and even a few older ones. As I walked through downtown Thessaloniki, not far from Aristotelous Square close to the sea, I walked past 4th-century monuments and wait ... what? ... yes, vendors selling Native American dreamcatchers. Young, contemporary Greeks call these oneiropagida (ονειροπαγίδα), yet they do not have a similar object from their own long forgotten, ancient, dream-focused culture. Evidence for this lost culture is found in museums nowadays. One man, who is in his 20s, shared two opposing views of today's Greek people. Dreams either mean little to nothing, he told me, or dreams must be interpreted, as they hold significance for some. For the latter group, oneirokritis (ονειροκριτης), or dream dictionaries, are popular. He considered those who used dream interpretation to be "superstitious," yet this term was not necessarily negative. The 21-year-old woman who was selling dreamcatchers, among other objects and souvenirs, told me that for her (and her friends), dreams were not meaningful. She said that her mother, however, carries a belief that night dreams are worth paying attention to and may take action if they seemed meaningful. This isn't a daily practice, though, as some dreams hold more weight than other dreams. A middle-aged cab driver from a small mountain town told me that contemporary Greeks today look at the old god and goddess culture as "fairy tales." That old mythology is not a part of the contemporary belief system whatsoever, he conveyed. With regard to dreams, he said that this is also mostly ignored, yet, for some Greeks, "powerful dreams" are given more attention. Those vivid or easily recalled types of dreams may need interpretation. The dream may be placed in one of two categories: good or bad. Dreams are judged, polarized. An example of a good dream, the cab driver told me, may involve flying, while a dream of a snake may be viewed as bad. I commented on how serpents were held in high regard in the past for their healing and transformative qualities. He agreed but said "times have changed." He attributed this shift in perspective to religious changes, particularly the rise of Christianity.

Thessaloniki's wonderful archeological museum staff provided stimulating discussion regarding the Greek history of dreaming. Two women working in the museum shop shared information about the healing nature of snakes as we looked at a marble relief being sold there, which features Asklepios. This 4th-century BCE relief depicts three stages of healing of a patient by the god Asklepios with two apotropaic eyes above. The healing ritual shown here appears to depict Asklepios giving injections and using snake venom as a healing substance. Snakes were his sacred servants. The original can be found in the sanctuary of Amphiaraos at Oropos (Attica). Apotropaic magic refers to the power to avert evil or harmful influences, bad luck, misfortune, or the evil eye. Its popularity is evident, even today, by the vast number of apotropaic amulets sold worldwide. Other copies of votive offerings to Asklepios also feature the serpent. Snakes can be found in numerous pieces of jewelry (bracelets and earrings in particular) worn by the ancient Greek and Macedonian peoples. The museum staff and I discussed how the serpent, or snake, was considered a strong healing, transformative force historically, yet with the arrival of Christianity, this all changed. From then on, snakes were primarily associated with women and evil, thus connecting the two. This myth connecting serpents, women, and evil continues to hold strong today.

One employee asked me to help her understand a puzzling dream of her own. I said that I would be honored to listen, but could not interpret another's dream, as I was not the author of it. She agreed that dreams belong to the dreamer and continued. In the dream, she was in her home and noticed many worms there. She took a broom and swept them out of her house right away. I noticed her contorted facial expression conveying disgust over the number of worms present in her dream. While worms can be positive for some, that was not the case with this woman. I reflected what I saw in her face and body posture, and she confirmed her negative perception of worms, along with her swift ability to remove them. I wondered aloud if she felt successful by her action, leading to the removal of all of the worms from her house. She smiled as her eyes widened, expressing thanks for my view on this dream, revealing a positive resolution in the end.

Dreams are fascinating. For this woman, her focus was on the negative feeling of worms, while for me, as a listener, her prompt action in the dream with successful resolution stood out immediately. Dreams belong to the dreamer, of course, and isn't it wonderful to have those that will listen and take them seriously? These exchanges offer fresh insights and perspectives.

FOUR

All at Once Time

For Australian Aboriginal peoples, The Dreaming *is all at once time*—it is the past, present and future all at the same time, yet beyond time. It is the eternal now. Dreamtime is primordial time, an encyclopedia of the world, a cosmic knowledge. There is no English equivalent. In The Dreaming all things exist at once. One need not wait for sleep or death to access this space. Instead, one can live the dreamtime in every moment. This is important because the song taught in The Dreaming teaches and protects the people.

> *"The distinction between past, present and future is only an illusion, however persistent."*—Albert Einstein (in a letter to Michelangelo Besso, 21 March 1955).

Due to the 600-plus Indigenous Australian groups (and nearly 3,000 dialects) originally, prior to European invasion, each with a diverse creation story, it is challenging to encapsulate this teaching in its totality, especially with the English language. Whether human (and all) existence was birthed by the rainbow serpent, the land, or another force, the songlines (Dreaming stories) with their immense lessons are everything, reflecting how we all share the same soul.

In the spring of 2020, Australian Aboriginal elder and senior law woman Grandmother Mulara spoke about how the COVID-19 pandemic appears to be more about fear than the virus. As earth is going through her vibrational shift, Grandmother Mulara tells us to "do something different." She asks, "How are we illiterate? Are we able to fend for ourselves?" She is therefore reminding us that we are not meant to be separate. We are meant to be in balance. We are meant to be in The Dreaming. "The Dreaming if a field of consciousness," she states, where we are not separate from each other, or animals, nature, environment—we are all one. Grandmother Mulara proclaims that it is time to ground ourselves and to connect with a totem. "Sing or hum to them—call in your totem." This is one way of connecting with Mother Earth. "Reconnect to nature because that's who you are." As the coronavirus continues to develop and spread globally, this is the time to carefully consider something: Who we are going to be on the other side of this? In closing she says, "Find your inner peace."

Shamanic initiation of Australian Aboriginal peoples, as well as other groups worldwide, may include ritual death in dreams or altered states of consciousness in caves or underground, depending on the specific group. Spirits or deceased souls remove the future medicine man's organs, replacing them with magical substances or new organs (Eliade, 2004). For the Arrernte, an Indigenous group of Australia, the sacred Dreamtime makes one into a healer through these types of experiences. In addition, the spirits gift the initiate with special stones which act as ceremonial healing tools for their patients (Kalweit, 1984). While COVID-19 has sadly led to the physical death of so many worldwide, how has it perhaps also led to another kind of death, a death more closely related to a spiritual nature such as individualism, ego, or self-centeredness?

Australian-American author Robert Moss survived a multi-year initiatory process as a young boy. At the tender age of three, Moss became very ill. Over the next eight years, he contracted pneumonia twelve times and was constantly around physicians, hospitals, drugs, and the like. During these years, he not only lived through cycles of sleeping and waking, but also in the liminal, or in-between, space—what Moss calls the twilight zone. At the age of nine, he was pronounced dead in a Melbourne hospital, only to come back with clear memories of another life. His family did not understand what he went through. Fortunately for young Moss, a friendship grew between him and an Aboriginal boy who validated all he had been experiencing. His new friend explained that one's spirit goes someplace else when the body gets sick, only to return once one gets well (Moss, 2014).

Moss speaks a great deal about the multi-dimensional universe, which he cleverly refers to as the "Multiverse." One way Moss helps dreamers to access the multiverse is by leading shamanic journeys with drumming. That's how we met—when I attended my first workshop. By going back inside a dream, consciously, to the particular environment, scene, or location, one can learn more and gain additional information needed for growth and understanding. Through this process of dream re-entry, we can change the past and future, according to Moss. We can travel back to our earlier self to help and heal. In March 2019, Moss offered an experiential through the Shift Network and I immediately knew that I wanted to understand more about the divinatory chart dream that I recalled from earlier that month. Moss led his listeners into an imaginal forest where a golden path emerged amidst the dense trees and foliage. He instructed us to walk down the path with our intention in mind (mine was clearly related to my health). I did so.

I met up with a bright light and also noticed Mountain Lion to my left side. Mountain Lion and I walk forward together a bit more, side by side. From this huge ball of bright light I am given a test tube filled with magical "elixir." I accept this gift. I take it and drink it immediately. The elixir is part liquid and part sparkling light, somewhat glittery. It is tasteless and pleasant to consume. I imagine it entering my body and projecting itself into my chest, breast, heart center. As I feel complete, I offer gratitude by kneeling to the light. Then, I turn around and retrace my steps along the golden path emerging from the forest. Mountain Lion follows me. As I begin to feel more and more grounded into my body, I emerge with tearful eyes and a sense of being thankful and humbled.

This vivid experience did not provide me with additional information on the details of the divinatory chart, but it did offer a healing drink offered up by a source that I knew was trustworthy. Perhaps this source thought it best to get on with it—time to heal, instead of revealing chart details that I may not have even understood. You never know what will come out of these imaginal experiences. I approach them with trust and an open heart. (More on dream re-entry later.)

Moss was one of the people who told me about Wanda Easter Burch. Burch is a long-term breast cancer survivor who wrote the

2003 book titled *She Who Dreams: A Journey into Healing through Dreamwork.* Her dreams saved her life. It was through her dreams that she diagnosed and healed herself—her dreams told her which treatments to accept. I was deeply curious about Burch's life since that time. Through ongoing email correspondence in the spring of 2020, Burch shared with me her beliefs about dreaming:

> In dreaming, which encompasses images from both ordinary reality and the sleep dream, we all receive powerful metaphors and imagery which can be used in useful exercises and self-dialogue to both understand our everyday dreaming and, in a healing environment, provide visual imagery for the healing journey, and empower the mind, spirit, and body. Dreaming is a continuing dialogue with the inner self, a constantly streaming two way message center, the inner voice—and inner physician in a time of healing—that speaks to us in sleep dreams or through the imagination, the voice that knows us best and allows us access once we relax and allow the day's intrusions to peel away.

During our correspondence, I asked about one specific dream that stood out for me because of its potency and power. Burch titled it *Field of Body Parts*—this dream can be found in her book *She Who Dreams*, yet she has allowed me to share it here as well.

> *I am in a large field, plowed in rows but sown with body parts. The parts are all new—they have grown like plants from the earth. They are sown by types, and each row of types is labeled. I am walking up and down the rows in the field, choosing new body parts to replace the old ones in my body. I choose a mask (a face), bones, muscles, blood veins, etc., until I have everything I need; and then I begin to put them all together. There are pots of herb mixtures, including hyssop, which are provided for me. I take the parts, each one individually, and dip them into the herb mixtures, cleansing each one thoroughly before placing it in my new body. Once my body is back together, I go to a kitchen where Ron and some friends are preparing vegetables, including potatoes, sour cream, and meat for the nourishment of my new body. Ron and my friends pour the vegetables and meat over large plates of grains, and I eat. Then I walk to the top of a hillside where there is a large gathering of people. Flyers are handed to the gathered people. I look down and there is a song printed ("Brightest and best are the sons of the morning....") on the flyer. We all begin to sing the song, and the words echo back and forth across the hillsides.*

This powerful dream is so alive, full of healing and nourishing energy! For Burch, it was quite rejuvenating and set the course for her next phase of healing.

Burch also shared information she presented in a paper at the 2008 IASD Psiber Dreaming Conference (an online conference for those interested in dreaming), along with more recent news of her life after cancer. She wrote,

> My journey did not end with my surviving breast cancer. In an amazing dream near the end of my treatments, I met an extraordinary guide who allowed me to re-negotiate my life contract. Part of the deal was that I was required to "give back." I began by serving on advocacy boards and talking to others about their own dreams of healing. I have collected hundreds of stories of diagnostic dreaming, healing imagery, and dream locales that have manifested in waking reality. I have witnessed people's lives transform in the presence of their dreaming and have witnessed people change their lives because they envisioned in their dreams a life much more suited to their healing and more confirming of their life purpose.
>
> The stories are everywhere, in every city and town in the world. There is no lack of personal confirmation that we have the ability to dream diagnostically for our bodies and that we have the ability to generate personal imagery for our healing and for the healing of others. We can vision the future for our health and pleasure; we can vision broader more expansive dreams for the health of our world once we perfect dreaming the health of our lives.
>
> We begin as individuals.

Two healing dream elements Wanda and I share are the drum and assistance from deceased family members. Post-diagnosis, we each became aware of the presence of a healing drum, and we each received support from female family members who had previously crossed over. The "tools" presented along the healing journey can be surprising. Burch added,

> Healing can be a creative journey; when it comes in a dream, healing imagery is a special gift. I am alive because I dream. My dreaming has led me to new experiences—a life of sharing and giving in a positive, appropriate manner, a life of exploring every day the vibrant confirming messages of life and purpose available to all of us in our dreams. This sharing and giving belongs to all of us, and communication with our

dreams can bring us together and present us tools for healing that can be both unique to our individual experience and common in the larger universe of dream diagnosis and healing.

Sometimes it is the person with the illness herself, and other times it is a healer in the community, as we will see in the next section on dreamwalking, who uses his or her dreams to diagnose a patient and make decisions regarding course of treatment.

Certain types of dreamwork can help those who are ill or approaching death, such as dream re-entry. Moss assists those in the dying process to go back into a dream in order to receive messages from the other side, ease disruptions or any fear of death, discover who might receive them, or learn the landscape of the new dimension about to be entered. That's right, we *can* explore the geography of the afterlife in dreams, because when we sleep, we enter a realm accessed by the deceased.

This type of soul travel, including sleep dreaming, can wake us up from the sleepwalking state. We can dream when asleep and when awake and in between. Robert Moss coined the term "Active Dreaming" for many reasons; one is as a response to hearing others talk about their dreams as if they are passive and were in the past, such as when he heard people say, "I had a dream." We have access to a source that is wiser than the ordinary mind. Dreaming can be utilized as a health practice—it is medicine, it is healing. Dreams diagnose what is going on inside the body every night. They show us how we feel about people and situations in addition to our physical state of functioning. We can begin to actively dream now—there is no need to wait for illness or disease development—and definitely there is no need to wait until end of life. At the same time, it is never too late to start on the road of dreaming with greater levels of consciousness. After all, what we discover about the nature of the "multiverse" may carry us onward with a sense of peace and fulfillment.

FIVE

Dreamwalking

A T ONE OF THE ANNUAL IASD conferences a few years back, the well-known American psychologist Stanley Krippner gave a presentation on shamanic dreamwalking. To become more familiar with the topic, we discussed dreamwalking at length the following year. Krippner said that "from a psychological perspective, shamans are socially-designated practitioners who obtain information from sources not ordinarily available to their peers." Shamans use this information for the benefit of their community. For shamans and traditional healers, dreams facilitate journeys to other worlds which then provide access to past and future events, inform a diagnosis of sickness, and allow for administration of prescribed cures. The latter may be done by dreamwalking, a process by which a shaman allegedly enters into a person's dream for benevolent purposes. Dreamwalking might also be employed to instruct, console, or to warn, Krippner conveys. A spirit guide may enter a shaman's dream for many of the same purposes.

In an earlier section of this book, I noted some of the initiatory processes as well as ways shamans have claimed to enter nonordinary states of consciousness, which Harner called a shamanic state of consciousness (SSC). In this section, I will say a bit about those shamans with whom Krippner has spoken, visited and spent time with, along with more on dreamwalking specifically.

Krippner spoke of shamans living in various parts of Indonesia as well as Rohanna (see her story below) and others. One of Krippner's students studied under a Blackfoot shaman for years. The Blackfoot tribal lands are in North America, spanning across part of the United States-Canada border. The student described many experiences of learning and gaining information in her dreams when her teacher (the Blackfoot shaman) would appear in them. Dreamwalking was one avenue for teaching his students. In the dream space he would give instruction and guidance for his students' spiritual development. Krippner also mentioned the well-known Igjugarjuk.

Famed northern Canadian Caribou Eskimo shaman Igjugarjuk received his call to shamanize in his youth through a series of dreams in which spirits held conversations with him. Igjugarjuk remained in a small hut during his shamanic training without food or drink (aside from a glass of water five days later and a scrap of meat over two weeks later). In total, he remained there, barely able to move, for 30 days. He was told to pray to the Great Spirit and to a helping spirit ally who would appear to him in a dream. This ally appeared, hovering in the air as advised and consoled him.

In the introduction to *The Power of Myth*, Bill Moyers wrote about a memory from a discussion with Joseph Campbell on human suffering as a major theme of classical mythology. Mortality is the cause of suffering—it "cannot be denied if life is to be affirmed," Campbell told Moyers. At this point in their conversation, Campbell relayed how it was Igjugarjuk who told the European visitors how true wisdom blooms out of suffering, opening "the mind to all that is hidden to others." Shamanic initiations and this particular path of service is not without hardship and often great suffering.

A close friend of Krippner, Rolling Thunder, was also reputed to be a shaman and dreamwalker. Another person who knew Rolling Thunder well said that if he wasn't feeling well, Rolling Thunder would come through in a dream and heal him in that dream. To learn more about him, I suggest reading the book *The Voice of Rolling Thunder: A Medicine Man's Wisdom for Walking the Red Road* by Jones and Krippner (2012). In that book, there is a chapter titled "Dreamwalking the Shamanic Way" that provides additional information on the phenomenon of dreamwalking.

All states (waking, trance, hypnagogia, hypnopompia, and dreaming) are equal, one just as "real" as the next, for the healer, shaman or medicine person who skillfully transitions through these states of consciousness with awareness, obtaining information not ordinarily available to community members. All of these states can be considered fluid, even overlapping, for healers, shamans or medicine people. These skilled practitioners consciously enter such states to access the past or future, obtain information from other worlds, diagnose illness, or administer treatment in order to help their community. Not only can dreamwalking allow for teaching and instruction to occur through the dream state, but by entering one's dream, a shaman might administer treatment so healing can take place.

A spirit ally or helper might walk into a shaman's dream for similar purposes. Such spirit guides can provide assistance and direction for the shaman. Often, it is such an introduction that places a person at the beginning of a long road toward a life of shamanism. As the person follows the calling, guides continue to make themselves known, providing teaching on how to heal with plants, sound and song, for example, as well as offering instruction on how to cure through specific rituals. As you can see, dreamwalking is not just for humans alone.

Typically, calls to shamanize are non-negotiable. For example, Torajan healer Rohanna Ler of Sulawesi's Tana Toraja region recalled dreams in which she was directed to begin a life as a traditional healer or shaman (Carpenter & Krippner, 1989). She initially ignored the dream messages yet eventually obliged many years later after her son was struck with blindness. In dreams and visions, spirits told her that she would be the one to cure her son; after all, becoming a healer was her fate, they told her, and visits to traditional and Western medical doctors did her son no good at all. The spirits showed her what she must do to heal her son's blindness, which she did. Soon after, her son fully recovered. Eventually, Rohanna became a known healer in her community. She reported that she often receives messages in dreams which provide information regarding what is needed to successfully treat her patients. Had she not followed the call to shamanize, further misfortune would likely have occurred (Carpenter & Krippner, 1989).

Since the 1980s, when Rohanna's healing practices were observed by Krippner, receiving treatment instructions in the dream state and practicing dreamwalking have not faded away.

Dreamwalking appears to be a timeless phenomenon. Both giving and receiving via dream are currently experienced and practiced today, by modern-day shamanic practitioners and highly skilled dreamworkers.

Clare Johnson provides instruction on healing others in dreams. In her 2017 book *Llewellyn's Complete Book of Lucid Dreaming: A Comprehensive Guide to Promote Creativity, Overcome Sleep Disturbances, and Enhance Health and Wellness*, she shares a practice for doing so (Practice #58). There are 10 steps in Johnson's practice "How to Carry Out a Lucid Dream Healing of Another Person" (2017, p. 290). I have not only condensed them here but have added my own twist:

- First, it is necessary to get permission from the person with the illness.
- Before going into a dream, choose your incantation of choice. This may be a word, a phrase or even a few sentences. This healing song can be combined with a movement or gesture.
- Now see yourself doing this and *believe.*
- Once you are dreaming, become lucid, aware.
- Locate the person in need of healing—the one whose permission you have already been granted. In this step, Johnson (2017) reminds us that this need not be literal, as we can send healing energy mentally with the expectation that it will reach the intended person.
- Stay focused with your intention, eliminating distraction, yet do not allow yourself to become so rigid as to not be open to the spontaneous. For example, your dream friend may have something important to tell you, or you might want to ask them a question about their illness in the dream.
- Now go for it—carry out the healing intent according to your plan.

As you come out of the dream after completing this mission, write everything down. Note all details. If you are able, contact the person with the illness and ask how they are doing. After, depending on your relationship, you might consider sharing the dream with them.

Shortly after I was diagnosed I asked several skilled dreamers I know for help by way of dreamwalking so that I could take in much needed healing energy beyond my own. Several were very gracious, offering help and support. Clare Johnson was one of them. A couple weeks later some of the dreamers told me they did healing work on my behalf, while others told me they planned to come find me in the dream space in order to help. While I did not recall all that made appearances in my dreams, I did recall some that did. They may have followed Johnson's 10-step practice, but not necessarily, as skilled dreamers have learned their own way of making things happen. With practice, you too will discover your unique approach.

During the Dreamwork Summit interview with Dr. Clare Johnson, she pointed out how dreams can range from being symbolic, reflecting symbolism, to being very direct and concrete. For example, being shown wearing a corset could represent restriction in one's life, while other dreams may deliver messages that are extremely direct, such as being told the location of a tumor hiding in one's body. Dr. Johnson claims that by being open to our dreams, we can invite healing into our life. This notion is the inspiration behind this book.

We also spoke about how, as dream workers, we do not tell people what their dreams mean; rather, we help dreamers unpack their own dreams and understand them for themselves. This brings us to an important point—dreamwalking or not, what a dream says to me does not reflect what a dream may mean to the one who had the dream. For example, my dream serpent is not your dream serpent. Mine helps and teaches. What does yours do?

Six

Sleep Yoga, Lucid Dreaming and Dream Yoga

JOHNSON AND I SHARE a love of yoga nidra and are experienced in the process thanks to our teachers. Yoga nidra supports dreamwork and can also bring harmony, deep contact with ourselves, and much needed healing. It helps to remember that transitional states of consciousness can also be considered "the dream"—we do not need to draw hard lines between these consciousness states. Those that easily move from wake to hypnopompia to light sleep, dream sleep, deep dreamless sleep, hypnogogia, back to waking state and daydreaming, all with conscious awareness, understand this well. Yes, those people might be a small population of monks, but it's good to know that with practice, anyone can increase awareness and wake up to the dream that is this life. Because contemporary Western culture views things linearly, we may be tempted to expect these states to line up and take place in the order listed. Do not be fooled. These states of consciousness do not necessarily occur in a linear fashion, and we can access various states of consciousness through different methods, such as shamanic journeying, hypnosis, and mediation. Furthermore, all states of consciousness are who we are, part of our life, and valuable, not just the intellectual thinking mind so overvalued by modern Western society. Let's move on to examine the practice known as yoga nidra.

Yoga Nidra

Yoga nidra is a sleep-based meditation, sometimes called yogic sleep. Essentially, yoga nidra is an ancient form of deep meditation which has been practiced for thousands of years. Nidra means sleep in Sanskrit, while yoga can translate to union. Most people in the West are only familiar with the style of yoga involving movement and body poses. That is asana, which is quite different from yoga nidra, the sleep-based meditation.

While brain waves decrease, one moves through the brain wave states associated with hypnosis (low alpha and theta) until much brain wave activity stops or becomes barely detectable (delta). However, the yoga nidra practitioner is conscious and aware and can respond to the person leading the experience. For example, the person participating in the yoga nidra may appear to be asleep, yet his or her body responds to requests made by the person leading the experiential exercise. Requests might be "Wiggle your fingers," "Place your arms on your stomach or chest," "Roll to the right side," and so on. For clarification, these requests are made at the end of the experience as a way to help the participant ease out of the practice.

For the entire year of 2019, I dove headfirst into yoga nidra and earned my certification in the Integrative Amrit Method of Yoga Nidra. Let me share my experience with you. In the winter of 2018–2019 I purchased an awesome book written by Kamini Desai of the Amrit Yoga Institute, *Yoga Nidra: The Art of Transformational Sleep*, what some have called "The Bible of Yoga Nidra." The deeper my investigation into yoga nidra, the more I wanted to learn. Shortly after purchasing the book, I saw that Desai would soon be leading a five-day Yoga Nidra immersion with John Vosler at Esalen Institute in Big Sur, California. Wanting an in-depth experience for myself, I enrolled immediately!

I arrived at Esalen on a Sunday, in the late afternoon, but early enough to settle in before the workshop officially kicked off. I say kicked off, but really it was a lovely slow-paced unfolding. If you have never been to Esalen, imagine the Garden of Eden, cliffside, and you'll get the idea. Soon enough, workshop attendees (myself included) were all on our backs, comfortably secure on our yoga mats with blankets or eye pillows. As the first taste of yoga nidra for the week was delivered, I rested deeply and allowed my thoughts to dissolve. A floaty sensation accompanying peaceful stillness, along with the sense of spaciousness, is deeply relaxing.

This is a space I have become familiar with from years of meditation, hypnosis, and conscious sleep-based practices I've been taught by Gnostic mystics, Taoists and Buddhists. Some of the particular breathing techniques, mantras, and visualizations were new and piqued my curiosity. I thought, "Well, Kim, welcome to the meditation limb of yoga." An important reminder was that no matter which spiritual lineage or framework the ancients originated from, the end result is that of knowing great peace and making contact with soul, regardless of the particular strategy applied. All used toning, visualizations, and the breath in some fashion or another, and while the precise technique differs from place to place across time, the end result is similar if not exactly the same. For me, this realization brings a sense of wholeness and humility and profound tranquility.

Over the next five days, attendees were taught core principles of yoga nidra and concepts concerning health and spirituality, including the subtle bodies, karma, and much more. We also learned how regenerative states and healing of the body are supported by yoga nidra, as the practitioner's brain waves slow down significantly, even down into delta brain wave states, during a yoga nidra practice. This is important because when we sleep each night, we only get about 20 minutes of delta—the most restorative brain wave state. By inducing yoga nidra for a short period during the day, we can add several additional minutes of the beneficial delta state, as the body sleeps while the mind remains conscious. This space is where healing suggestions can be incorporated—here the mind-body complex responds without having to do anything. What a delight this immersive workshop was, especially due to the class receiving two yoga nidras each day—one in the morning and another in the afternoon. All stressors seemed to melt away as each day passed. After a yoga nidra session, which are typically 30–45 minutes in length, I feel so comfortably relaxed, focused and recharged. I walk away with the firm knowledge that my body has been given the gift of additional support and good care.

In this fast-paced world with its many demands and easy access to a slew of mind-numbing distractions, I believe we are in desperate need of quality restoration and time and space to ground ourselves, breathe, and connect with ourselves and those around us. What better way to prioritize our health every day than with yoga nidra? Utilize this a few afternoons a week—it's like a healing power nap!

Lucid Dreaming

As much as I'd like to jump ahead to sharing my thoughts about dream yoga, I'll back up so I can say a little more about lucid dreaming first. No discussion of dreams is complete without allowing for some exploration of lucid dreaming—that is, when the dreamer is aware that he or she is dreaming. Stephen Laberge and Howard Rheinhold grabbed the attention of Westerners with their 1990 book *Exploring the World of Lucid Dreaming.* At this time, lucid dreaming has become so popular that one can easily find online summits and courses on the topic ranging from the basics to complex lucid dreaming phenomena. I recently attended the online summit titled the Many Worlds of Lucid Dreams sponsored by the IASD. There, I was exposed to a wide variety of lucid dreaming discussions which emerged from the papers and videos presented by the instructors, from lucid art to lucid healing and beyond.

Over the past 20-some years I have witnessed this topic of lucid dreaming go from being completely misunderstood and viewed as dangerous (I'm recalling old undergrad friends and our discussions during the mid–1990s) to being hailed as the way to overcome just about any obstacle known to humankind. Sure, lucid dreaming has a respectable range of benefits and applications and can happen spontaneously at any age. For some, it comes naturally, but it can also be taught—basically, it is a learned skill. Research suggests that combining several of the popular lucid dream induction techniques is effective (Aspy et al., 2017). We can all learn how to increase or lengthen states of heightened awareness and maintain consciousness for longer and longer periods of time as brain waves slow down. Lucid dreaming just takes some practice.

When it comes to lucid dreaming, the question of safety some-times arises. There is nothing dangerous about this practice since we dream every night, even when we may not remember doing so. For those that have a fair level of dream recall, I ask, "When it comes to dreaming safely, would it really matter whether our awareness was at a lower degree versus higher degree?" Probably not. As it is with most skills, it is wise to learn how to navigate unfamiliar terrain. How unfamiliar is it really, knowing that we dream every night? Unfortu-nately, even though humans dream each night, we are usually not aware of that fact in the moment it is taking place. Are you dreaming now? How do you know?

When one has a particular degree of lucidity in a dream, he or she can use that time to practice motor skills. That's because the neural mechanisms are the same whether the movement occurs in the dream or the physical waking state. The same is true for imag-ined movement or movements rehearsed in hypnotic states. Can the practice of lucid dreaming be utilized as an "effective tool in sports practice"? Some researchers would claim this is the case, especially if dream distractions are minimal (Schladlich et al., 2017). How simi-lar that is to the waking state, in that distractions do not help us there either.

What other skills could be practiced and enhanced when done while one is dreaming? Perhaps one group of skills would be less con-crete and measurable such as the practice of healing arts. We have just touched the tip of the iceberg. This type of research spawns so many more questions. I am so excited to see what future research can tell us about our innate capacities for performance in dreams!

Lucid dreaming, while often focused on self-improvement, is more common than most people think. Lucidity exists along a spec-trum, from minor degrees of awareness to fuller, heightened states of awareness. Waking up in a dream the very first time is truly a signifi-cant life experience—it's often unforgettable. That was the case my first few times. They were nothing like what I was used to or would even expect. People behave in different ways while lucid. Some peo-ple choose to control their dream content if they are able, while oth-ers use their conscious dream episodes to make discoveries about the nature of existence. The choice is yours to some degree—we all operate with different agendas and belief systems. Life experience, age, culture, opportunity, and who we spend our time with can determine how we proceed along this path. The lucid dream journey is not one size fits all. Our firsthand experiences and the direct knowledge gained in the vast world of dreams, and other nonordinary states of consciousness, influence how we practice and the level of dedication. In my early experiences, I just went along, witnessing everything! Later, as I became a more serious student of conscious dreaming (and even later shamanic journeying), I began to fly myself to diverse geographical locations, some that exist in this physical reality, and some that only exist in other realms—a space not perceived in the ordinary waking state through the major senses.

No matter our history, lucid dreaming can be used as a vehicle for exploring reality, even life and death itself. Through this exploration, we may discover the subjective nature of both the dream state and the waking state. Tibetan Buddhist literature claims that the clear light, like the light that arises at the time of death, can also be experienced at the moment of falling asleep. Moreover, the dream state is like a post-death state (bardo), "since in dreams one often conceives of oneself in a body and undergoes vivid experiences that are creations of mind, just as beings in the bardo do. Waking from a dream is similar to rebirth, since the illusory dream body passes away and we awaken to a new 'reality.' Because of these similarities, dream yoga is said to be an important method for gaining control over the production of mental images, a skill that is extremely useful." For more on this rich topic, see chapter 10 of John Power's 1995 book *Introduction to Tibetan Buddhism* and the PBS Frontline page https://www.pbs.org/wgbh/pages/frontline/shows/tibet/understand/dying.html.

In addition, lucid dreaming (dreaming while knowing that you are dreaming) is often used for entertainment and pleasure. This learnable skill has become quite popular in the past several years among a diverse group of individuals, from students to professionals. Many of those new to lucid dreaming are thrilled to learn that they can control their dreams and do what they most desire.

Overindulging in sweets and fatty fast food, racing expensive cars, beating up enemies larger than oneself, having sex with supermodels (or becoming one), you name it, I've heard it all. Well, probably not, but those were the top responses I recall coming from my undergraduate psychology students. These lucid dream experiences made going to sleep exciting for them. To each semester's half-dozen or so lucid dreamers, I would say, "Wow, that's something." It was something, as I didn't expect to meet so many who attended to their dream lives. Then I would ask the experienced students about less conventional matters. Had they ever talked to a deity or wise person, transported themselves to a sacred site, or asked to be shown what death is like or how to prepare for it? The responses were mostly blank stares or contorted faces. A few scratched their heads as they muttered, "Nope." I left it at that. These university psychology majors may have been unaware of all they could learn through making the most of their nocturnal lucid experiences.

As popular as it has become, lucid dreaming is nothing new. Former professor and Episcopal clergyman Morton Kelsey authored *God, Dreams, and Revelation: A Christian Interpretation of Dreams.* In his 1991 revised and expanded edition, as well as his 1974 edition of the book, Kelsey reminds us of the large variety of parapsychological and other influential dreams recorded in Saint Augustine's writings, particularly in his correspondence with Evodius (Kelsey, 1991, p. 136). Below, Kelsey relays what is believed to be the first recorded lucid dream in Western history. One of Augustine's writings (a letter from 415 CE) highlights an impactful experience for Gennadius, a physician, who reported a series of notable dreams, which revealed the nature of consciousness, death and the afterlife. In the dreams, Gennadius carries out dialogue with a dream figure. In one of Gennadius' dreams, the dream companion asserts, "but I would have you know that even now you are seeing in sleep," which prompts Gennadius to become lucid (Kelsey, 1991, pp. 240–241). The lucid dream continues until Gennadius grasps an understanding that life and perceptive faculties continue after the death of the physical body. In the end, the dream figure instructs him to let go of any doubts he has regarding life after death. Augustine claims that the doubts previously held by Gennadius vanished as a response to his nocturnal lucid experiences. Dreams, especially lucid ones, can be that powerful!

What one does in the dream state affects both body and brain. You can train your physical body by what you do in the dream state. We know this from scientific studies. Training in singing, art, athletics, and solving mathematical puzzles are some examples of purposeful, induced lucid dream activities practiced in order to improve waking life experience or events. This is a popular reason for learning the hows and whys of lucid dreaming today. I'm sure it's clear that the experience of dreaming lucidly can lead to self-satisfaction and self-fulfillment (remember my students?). In addition, trauma survivors and military veterans have been taught to lucid dream for therapeutic purposes, as a way to alleviate PTSD symptoms. What a powerful modality to support healing! What's more, anyone can use lucid dreams to ask specific questions about diagnostic information and best avenues for healing. It was December 2019 when I woke up in a dream and recalled my intention to ask about the cause of the chronic illness I had been managing along with what my body needed to heal from the condition. I called out to the dream, asking two questions. "Dreaming mind, how do I heal this condition?" The lucid dream space shifted and I found myself in a black void. There in front of me was a white silhouette of a woman sitting, hovering in lotus position. I then asked, "Dreaming mind, what is the root cause of this condition?" Suddenly, an alien-like face appeared. This startled me out of the dream space, so I woke up then. I logged this dream and eventually painted it. The painting is hung in my home as a reminder to use the calm, centering space of meditation as a way to soothe my nervous system and support my immune system. As for the face that was shown, I wondered if a foreign virus had been the cause. After all, I was living a fast-paced lifestyle up until just a few years ago, finding myself chronically exhausted. Perhaps my immune system had given up and hadn't been able to fight off what it normally would have if I had lived more harmoniously. The wonders of lucid dreaming have impact, meaning and purpose, sometimes lasting a lifetime, yet remains relatively secular and focused on the self among contemporary Westerners.

In her 2017 book *Llewellyn's Complete Book of Lucid Dreaming,* Clare Johnson writes, "Lucid dreaming does not always involve deliberate dream control." Nor must it involve manipulation. We can remain open when lucid and go with the flow. Andrew Holecek (2016), in his book *Dream Yoga: Illuminating Your Life Through Lucid Dreaming and the Tibetan Yogas of Sleep,* describes "witnessing" dreams as a "type of lucid dream where you prefer not to engage in the dream. You're lucid, but you prefer to just watch what unfolds without changing anything."

Dream Yoga

"Dream yoga picks up where lucid dreaming leaves off," says Holecek (2016). Self-transcendence is what dream yoga is all about. It is a spiritual practice, more so than a psychological one, essentially. In Buddhist and Hindu worldviews, there is the concept of life as *maya,* a dream, viewing life as illusory. Maya is Sanskrit for illusion. Dream yoga's purpose is to wake us up from the dream or illusion. As one's practice grows and develops, worldly things may start to lose their power, and waking and dream worlds come to be viewed as equally real or unreal.

When I watched Tenzin Wangyal Rinpoche speak about dream yoga on the Jung Platform, an online education space for psychology and spirituality, I was touched by several of his points. He described dream yoga as the wisdom, realizations, knowledge and experiences related to dream. Yoga is knowledge or awakened state, he said. Tenzin Wangyal Rinpoche explained ways of looking at dream yoga in the Tibetan Buddhist tradition.

Everything is like a dream. The waking state is like a dream. There is nothing out there the way you are seeing it. There is nothing out there that you think is out there. There is nothing there. This is a dynamic, energetic field in which you are perceiving your own reality ... in which you are able to project. You are basically seeing yourself in this infinite possibility field of light and energy. You are projecting yourself. It's like a dream. This reality is not more real than the dream. The dream reality is not less unreal than this reality. These two realities are connected to each other very well. The practice of dream yoga is to awaken the unconscious in your dream by practicing in these waking life experiences— it's the same. Real dream yoga practice takes place in the day when we are learning—the exam comes at night. The experiences in the night are caused by the conditions and experiences of the day. We practice during the day, in the waking state, in order to pass the exam in the dream state [Tenzin Wangyal Rinpoche, free online presentation on the Jung Platform; January 17, 2021].

For the practice of dream yoga, we use our body as a tool, or vehicle, for growth. Consistency in practice matters, which is the case for any discipline. Holecek's (2016) book offers chapters on both Western and Eastern lucid dream induction techniques, thus reminding us that we can become our own instructor, teaching ourselves how to do this stuff! My teachers taught a combination of both Western and Eastern induction techniques for the purpose of conscious dreaming, which I began practicing regularly. As a deeply curious student, I wanted to engage with my dreaming world in new ways. After a few months of dedication to the set of daily exercises, I met my initial goal. Overzealous, I added more techniques to my daily routine and set new goals. On one hand, I began gaining increasing levels of competence. On the other hand, like other spiritual or health-based practices in my life, I became inconsistent and distracted. Later, realizing that I had lost time, I set lofty goals, which led to feeling frustrated and pressured. Disillusioned, I gave up for a time. This happens to some of us—it can be considered normal human activity. The moral of the story is to monitor the ego and to be gentle and kind to oneself while making daily commitments and not set deadlines or unrealistic goals that are in opposition to a preferred long-range lifestyle choice.

As we develop along our psychospiritual path, we may want to bring a waking life practice into the dream state. When dreaming lucidly, try engaging in a form of meditation. What happens? Holecek (2016) claims that "the meditation you accomplish in the dream state is up to 9 times more effective and more transformative than what you do in the waking state." So why not? Even in fully lucid dream states, where we have control and clear decision-making capacity (such as making the decision to meditate), we may come into contact with the unexpected. For example, in most dreams (even lucid ones) people often run away from their disowned aspects (think powerful, hideous monsters). "Dreams are truth-tellers," writes Holecek in his article "The Art of Lucid Dreaming" published in *Conscious Lifestyle Magazine*. He adds, "Dream yoga will show you a great deal about who you are, and where you stand." In dream yoga, integration of our unwanted, split-off parts is one way to go. In this example, we turn toward (a monster, in this case) instead of away. At the very least, we do not resist. By doing so we can gain awareness, illumination and transformation through acceptance. Some dreamers turn toward the scary creature and ask a question. "What do you represent?" or "What do you need?" are examples. Others simply remain with the experience. By clearing out the cobwebs, or moving deeper into the monster's lair, we have an opportunity to tap into a deeper core, a greater awareness.

Due to the conscious awareness in this dream state, which becomes more common with practice, we can do much more, such as fly, manipulate the body, transform into an animal, converse with a deity, pass through seemingly solid objects, practice tai chi or qi gong, meditate, and more. As one moves along the dream yoga path, exercising greater levels of spiritual discipline is evermore encouraged, and this is where deeper meditation practices come into the picture. This is another area where I struggle and stir. Once the fun has been had, the simple curiosities expunged, and the egoic explorations complete, the mind is often pulled toward more of the same. This pattern is a way for me to see my own inner distractions as well as face the part of me that fears thinning the self, not wanting to wake up from the perpetual dream called life (a serious question!). With further growth, trust, gentle practice and dedication, plus a little patience, this too shall pass.

There is much to be gained. Through these practices of the night, we can bring those insights into our day-to-day lives. By gaining mastery nocturnally, we can take the driver's seat in our own mind, thus decreasing the unconscious controlling our life.

In early 2018, I spoke with Joseph Dillard about his 40-plus-year psychotherapy practice and his understanding of dream yoga. Dillard told me that he believes dreaming to be "our most misunderstood and underutilized, innate capability." He begins by summarizing some core points. In the Buddhist and Hindu traditions, life is seen as a dream. Yoga, as a psychospiritual discipline, can wake us from an existence of perpetual sleepwalking. The Buddhist and Hindu worldviews are derived from shamanism, which, in some cases, assumes a fundamental cosmological dualism—that is, an underworld of demons and devils and an overworld of angels and deities. In other shamanic conceptualizations, "low spirits" can be redeemed, unlike the demons and devils of organized religions. Trance and dreaming allow shamans to access communication with these worlds. Shamanistic approaches to dream yoga are concrete and literal; what you experience in a dream is a reality in another dimension. Most traditional approaches, whether they are Amer-Indian shamanistic, Siberian, Hindu, Buddhist, or Tibetan Buddhist approaches, will focus on the objective concreteness of experiences and further divide dreaming into either spiritual or mundane categories. You'll find that again and again wherever you look at them.

This traditional approach to dreamwork and dream yoga is in opposition to the Western psychological approach, which sees everything in a dream or interior, psychological experience, as a self-aspect, sub-personality, or "shadow." Dillard adds that these two approaches generate a fundamental division in approaches to dreamwork, with the first tending to view dreams as either sacred, spiritual, and highly meaningful or secular, profane, and meaningless, while the second emphasizing ownership and the self-created nature of experience in order to foster responsibility and personal empowerment.

According to Dillard, Tibetan dream yoga is divided into two different categories—one is the category associated with the great Tibetan yogi Milarepa, which emphasizes gaining power to awaken from samsara, or the clinging to the cycle of birth, death, and rebirth, by waking up in your dreams. In this way, lucid dreaming becomes a tool for waking up. Dillard states, "The idea is to wake up in your waking life. You can rehearse this and learn how to do it by waking up in a dream, to realize that you are dreaming, and have various experiences which will teach you that you have control. Consequently, you'll start to wake up in your waking life and to differentiate the dream-nature, the illusory-nature of waking life from dream life." The Milarepa approach focuses on the steps or injunctions of the yoga of waking up while you are dreaming.

The second Tibetan dream yoga category is known as Tibetan deity yoga. In short, with this approach, one meditates on a wise being (bodhisattva) or the Buddha and internalizes a mandala in addition to many other details, recalling colors, shapes, and figures, for example, in order to embody and become the deity. One tries to fuse with or become the consciousness of the deity, Dillard explains. In Tibetan deity yoga, this work uses sacred elements from the Tibetan Buddhist tradition. The distinction between sacred and secular (whether in dream or waking or meditative states) is apparent, as it is in the shamanic traditions. For a more in-depth discussion of these two types of Tibetan dream yoga, see my resources list.

When we are aware in the dream and work toward dream yoga mastery, we start to understand the dream-like quality of the waking state. Those "masters who have accomplished dream yoga, and truly see the world as a dream, can manipulate the physical world as if it is no longer physical," writes Holecek (2016, p. 247). This has serious implications for one's health and healing.

SEVEN

Hypnosis

Hypnosis is a unique state of consciousness. When I am in a hypnotic state, I feel very relaxed. This is shared by many, but not all, people. On the surface it may appear similar to yoga nidra, yet brain research shows that it is an entirely different state. Specifically, one passes through hypnotic states on the way to yogic sleep. Hypnosis is sometimes referred to as a trance state. Hypnotherapy may be thought of as the therapeutic use of hypnosis. This can be done alone. That's right, with self-hypnosis, you can apply it on yourself. What better way to bring about relaxation! We can even program positive intentions and affirmations into our own subconscious mind. Later in this chapter, you'll find two short versions of self-hypnosis that can be utilized when there is little spare time, such as in your car on a lunch break or after the kids are finally asleep.

First, let me tell you about Shirley McNeal, licensed psychologist and clinical hypnotist, whom I had the pleasure of interviewing in April 2020. She has been practicing for almost 50 years as a professional and is an incredible source of scientific and clinical knowledge. McNeal had a lot to share when it comes to hypnosis—especially its relationship to dreaming and its healing effects. In an email exchange she wrote, "I believe hypnosis and dreaming are similar in that both deal with the unconscious mind and states of altered consciousness. While dreaming, except for lucid dreaming, is almost completely beyond our conscious control, hypnosis can deal with unconscious processes, and be more under our control in terms of choosing to go in and out of trance states, especially when a hypnotist and subject are involved."

During our video chat, I asked McNeal to share her thoughts

about bringing hypnosis and mindfulness together. She explained that many professionals bring the two together because they can be combined so well. McNeal stated, "Hypnosis and mindfulness go very well together. Mindfulness also involves a trance state that is very similar in its characteristics to the trance state of hypnosis, which is also very similar to the hypnagogic or hypnopompic phenomena of dreaming. All three of those areas, or altered states, share a similar kind of trance state where a person's attention is very narrowed and focused. We can induce ourselves, going into these states at will."

She continued, "Some professionals are using Mindfulness-Based Cognitive Hypnotherapy [MBCH] which is a merging of mindfulness practice with cognitive therapy and hypnosis." MBCH was initially developed by Assen Alladin for treating depression but was later used for several other conditions. When asked about some distinctions, McNeal said, "With mindfulness you're more focusing on internal states while with hypnosis you can be focused internally as well as being receptive to what's happening externally in terms of the person who is inducing hypnosis." In addition, cognitive therapy encourages an external orientation—that is, an ability to go outside of oneself to use information to form responses that are more adaptive (Yapko, 2011). This brought to mind my own thoughts on how there are many altered states of consciousness known by different names. At the same time, they all share similarities reflecting a fluidity. Hypnosis, for example, is a right brain dominant phenomenon while in self-hypnosis (a lighter state of hypnosis) the left-brain is involved as well. I recalled learning how with yoga nidra activation occurs in both hemispheres. Still, the states share many similarities. McNeal added that "there are some differences between meditation and hypnosis" as well as similarities. Guided imagery also overlaps these areas and can be used as part of the induction process. We still have a lot to discover, I thought, as she pointed out that all the variables involved can make the neuropsychological research challenging. What we do know is that when it comes to meditation and hypnosis, the neurophysiology is similar (Yapko, 2011). Guided mindfulness meditation and clinical hypnosis share great similarity "in the way they focus attention, each giving rise to similar qualities of experience that people describe as different from usual consciousness … a sense of detachment, timelessness, and absorption in the experience" are not uncommon qualities (Yapko, 2011, p. 121).

The part of our mind that is associated with action, executive control and a subjective sense of control is referred to as the ego. A component of psychotherapy involves empowerment and strengthening the ego. These individually tailored ego-strengthening interventions are meant to increase a person's ability to "access resources from within one's inner world" leading to the experience of increased strength, adequacy, and coping both internally and externally (McNeal, 2020, p. 395). Ego-strengthening interventions, whether ranging from direct and highly structured to indirect and unstructured, pair well with hypnosis and self-hypnosis.

McNeal told me about one of her clinical cases from many years ago. She recalled one young man who had done "talk therapy" in the past and was ready to try hypnosis. He also paid attention to his dreams and recorded them all, seeing them as sources of help and support. This client was dealing with severe social anxiety, making it hard for him to leave the house or interact with others. He also had a lot of food allergies, avoided restaurants out of fear, and was very thin. Other conflicts involved how to work and earn money as well as other practical kinds of issues.

> [The] social anxiety was the main focus of treatment, and with hypnosis and ego-state therapy he looked at the different parts of himself—three ego states were isolated and identified. One part was called "social"— this part wanted a social life, to have a girlfriend and get out to meet people. The second identified part (supernatural) was mystical and wise. Then there was a third part of himself (ascetic) who really wanted to stay in with his own thoughts, his own writings and do artwork, and not have to bother with other people at all. These three parts were in a great deal of conflict most of the time. In hypnosis we were able to isolate and talk to each of these parts to see how their functions might be altered to accomplish more of what he really wanted to do and how these parts could work together more harmoniously. Then he began having dreams where these different parts would occur in his dreams in different forms, particularly the social part. In his dreams, it was that part that was going out, having fun, dating, and having a social life, while

the ascetic one wanted to retreat into a cave in the mountains. In time, it was very interesting how his dream life and the hypnosis work became integrated.

This type of therapy was helpful in that this client started going out more and experimented gradually with seeing how much he could do before becoming anxious. He continues to record his dreams and attend to the suggestions that come up in those dreams. Hypnosis sessions were reduced in place of dreamwork. The dream provides feedback. Positive progress continues in all areas of his life where there had once been concern.

Hypnosis is not all rainbows and butterflies. Entering this state can allow things we don't want to see about ourselves to come to light. For example, resentments, feelings of uncertainty, and buried truths can all surface. If we refuse to acknowledge or name these, they may develop into physical symptoms during or after a hypnotic trance. McNeal recalled a pregnant couple she had worked with in the past. After a hypnosis session for labor, delivery and bonding, the non-pregnant partner complained of a severe headache, which was unusual. This led to facing an unacknowledged truth—the ambivalence he had about the pregnancy and had kept secret from his pregnant partner. We may never know the depth of this man's ambivalent feelings. After all, we cannot notice what we choose to not notice.

Self-Hypnosis

Several experts recognize the value of self-hypnosis (Banyan & Kein, 2001) as well as the "individual differences in responsiveness to any approach" (Yapko, 2011). Dr. McNeal had some ideas to share about self-hypnosis as well. In an email, she wrote,

> Self-hypnosis can be extremely helpful in many ways. A light hypnotic trance is very similar to the trance state that occurs during meditation, and can be very relaxing as well as insight-inducing. There are studies showing that self-hypnosis recordings made for patients, that they listen to regularly for several weeks, can have profound effects, especially when these are recordings specifically tailored to the specific patient,

created by the therapist with whom a successful therapeutic alliance has been formed. There are methods of self-hypnosis that are very useful for relaxation and stress reduction that patients can learn to use in the moment. For example, one very brief self-hypnosis method that I teach can be done anywhere at any time for anxiety reduction. I believe the most effective use of self-hypnosis can occur when an individual seeks out a well-trained licensed professional who will work with the person hypnotically and create a recording that the person can then use on his or her own, helping to extend and amplify treatment effects.

For many reasons, I agree with her point that connecting with a licensed professional is very important.

Self-hypnosis can be achieved in various ways. McNeal demonstrated one method developed by a psychiatrist who uses hypnosis. She said to think of the count of three—each number paired with a movement or action. On the count of one, roll your eyes upward as if you are trying to look at your eyebrows. On two, you take a deep breath in while closing your eyes. And on three, exhale while you let your head relax and imagine yourself floating. Then slowly open your eyes. With familiarity and a little practice, this simple technique can be done just about anywhere without anyone noticing. "You can feel this kind of up-down internal feeling that comes as one continues to practice," McNeal says. It's that quick and that subtle. The relaxation response quickly sets in. It is not necessary, but the person can recite an intention or affirmation at that point if desired. Repetition is key. While there are many general recordings out there, McNeal reminds us that "there is a consensus in the field among professionals that the best recordings are tailor-made, specific to the individual" and his or her unique goals.

McNeal continues, "People can involuntarily experience self-hypnosis, however, during periods of reverie, dissociation, and sometimes during traumatic experiences. An example would be times when you might have been driving, daydreaming, and drive by your exit without noticing it until later. There is the phenomenon of hypnotic dreaming whereby the therapist might induce a hypnotic trance in a patient and suggest having a dream about the solution to a particular problem. Upon re-alerting, the patient usually can recall the dream and describe how it relates to the problem." How wonderful, I thought. Now that's some magical dream medicine!

If you do not have access to a licensed professional, one with additional credentials in clinical hypnosis as McNeal does, you can still try some things at home as she explained above. Here, I'll share with you a part of my process. Before trying it out, ask yourself, "What is my highest intention at this point in my life?" It could be almost anything—to live a healthy lifestyle, to feel calmer and at peace, to attract a suitable partner, to release anxiety and worries, you name it. Once you have the general intention noted, list some supporting affirmations underneath your heading. For example, I often focus on maintaining health, so if that is my primary intention, some of my supporting affirmations might be:

- Only healthy cells live in this body.
- My organs function optimally.
- I'm an automatic self-healer, I'm healing myself right now.

Whatever you choose, write them down. Now you are ready to go on to the next step.

There are some safe and simple ways to slow down our own brain waves at will. First and foremost, turn out the lights if it is daytime so that only natural light comes through the windows. If it is night, a lamp with soft lighting is fine. Just don't use bright overhead lighting. Next, find a comfortable place to lay down. Reclining in a comfortable chair or in your car works too. Begin to focus on your breathing. This brings on relaxation naturally. From there, count down from 10 to one, inserting short phrases in between random numbers while continuing to breath deeply. Such as "ten, nine, relaxing more now, eight, seven, six, heavy, loose and limp, five, fully relaxed, four, three, so comfortable, effortless, two, going even deeper now, one, so calm and peaceful." At this point, relaxation and a low alpha brain wave is likely achieved, so it is time to insert that affirmation. I'll use one of my earlier examples: "I'm an automatic self-healer, I'm healing myself right now." As I say this, I imagine healing energy flowing to the place that needs healing. It could be to bring relief from a headache or to bring nurturing to an injury, for example. *See the healing happening* in the present moment. Gently bring your thumb and index finger together as a signal to your mind, anchoring the intention. Offer a word of thanks for what is happening now. Continue to breathe. Notice any images, memories, or even perceived auditory messages that may come. When you feel complete, count up from one to five and insert a phrase somewhere in the middle such as "feeling more awake and aware." On five, wiggle your fingers and toes, then gradually open your eyes. This is an example of how self-hypnosis can be utilized with limited time. These practices should be consistent but do not need to be lengthy.

Now that we've covered a little on the topics of yoga nidra, lucid dreaming, dream yoga, and self-hypnosis, it should be clear that these can all be used for wellness and health purposes. I use them all, but others may find one application is most comfortable and effective. Play around—try things out. To get the most out of the technique of choice, I suggest sticking with it for several months before moving on to another technique. The choice is yours and I hope that you find one that fits perfectly into your personal medical bag of tricks.

Eight

Intuitive Development

INTUITION—IT'S A MESSY CONCEPT. I believe the term intuition refers to an evolutionary, life-promoting sixth sense sometimes called "a gut feeling." For some, intuition arrives as a felt sense, for others, it is auditory, like an inner voice, and for others, intuition manifests visually, where imagery is experienced. The *American Psychological Association Dictionary of Psychology* defines intuition as "immediate insight or perception, as contrasted with conscious reasoning or reflection." No matter what, many people report being guided and making decisions based on their intuition. A female may claim "women's intuition," yet all humans are intuitive regardless of sex or gender identity. One culture-bound stereotype asserts that women may be more tapped in to their intuitive knowing because they seem to tend to their feeling states more often or more deeply than men do. The roots of this may be social and cultural, as noted. Either way, I'm sure you've heard these stereotypes. Intuition, however, has its foundation in the body itself, and we will cover that next. But before we cover neural correlates, I'll offer a few more thoughts on the definitions and concepts surrounding intuition. In her 2011 article "Viva las Vagus," Dr. Jennifer F. Tantia reminds us that most cognitive science definitions of intuition describe the phenomenon as unconscious, nonlinear, illogical, nonverbal or irrational. This, she says, results in negative conceptions and does not highlight intuition's connection to the body. Tantia writes, "I suggest that intuition as an immediate embodied experience is also recognized through non-verbal knowledge that cannot be traced to an emotional pattern or memory" (2011, p. 30). In Tantia's 2014 publication "Is Intuition Embodied?" she notes opposing conceptions—misconceptions, really—which align intuition with emotional insight, body language, and psychic phenomenon. As a trained body psychotherapist and somatic psychologist, Tantia calls attention to the notion that intuition is often used during therapy sessions, yet it is "the most misunderstood tool in a therapist's skillset" (2014, p. 211). For more information on the embodied intuitive experience, see Tantia's publications, videos, or website.

The Nervous System

In an attempt to further understand intuition and the body, let's turn our attention to nerves and their systems. The cranial nerves originate in the brain. There are twelve of them and they travel through the body at some distance. Not all cranial nerves are equal. The tenth cranial nerve, known as the vagus nerve, is of particular interest here because it runs between the brain and the gut as well as to other organs with its many branches. The vagus nerve provides sensory, motor and autonomic functions of the viscera (glands, digestion and heart rate). When one gets a "gut feeling" or hunch from deep within his or her core, torso or chest, the vagus nerve may be a key player. This important cranial nerve running from the brain downward has not just one plexus but several, even as far down in our body as the colon and small intestine. A plexus is like a bundle or network of nerves. Some describe the information gathered from these nerve bundles as intuition, whether that is a felt sense of danger lurking, an inner voice prompting us to run, or an image flashing through our mind's eyes showing us what to do or what is to come.

Some people have noticed the similarity of the locations of each vagus nerve plexus compared with the locations of the main chakras that yogis say run vertically through the body from the head to the base of the spine. This is also similar in location to the central meridian in the body, according to traditional Chinese medicine, which runs vertically as well. No matter which medical system you feel most comfortable with, recognize the similarities. I cannot explain what might be taking place for someone who gets intuitive hunches in their calves or pinky toe, but it sure isn't rocket science to see how we can perceive information uploaded from and within the viscera. This tells me that the brain is very important but not the big boss after all. In a similar fashion, the heart sends signals to the brain, but for so long, scientists believed it was only the other way around. Our organs, nerves, and brain form a multi-way communication system. The brain is not the only one sending out messages. Now that we know this, we can work with other locations in the body to further develop our intuition.

First, let me explain the autonomic nervous system (ANS), as it must be included in any discussion about the vagus nerve or viscera. The ANS has three parts—the enteric, the sympathetic and the parasympathetic. The enteric, sometimes called the intrinsic nervous system, is a complex system of 100 million nerves that regulate digestive activity. The enteric system transmits and processes messages in addition to other functions. The sympathetic nervous system is responsible for action, such as defending ourselves or running away from danger, so blood pressure increases, digestion slows down, and the heart beats faster, while the parasympathetic is like putting on the brakes—resting and digesting, for instance. Here, pulse rate decreases, blood pressure slows, and food can be digested. The ANS is always working so that our body's internal functions behave normally.

Regulation

The parasympathetic nervous system and the vagus nerve do not exist in isolation. If we lead a lifestyle where we are constantly activated, from a nervous system point of view, it is almost impossible to remain fully embodied and tune in to our deeper ways of knowing. We can stimulate parasympathetic activation through the vagus nerve by simply taking deep abdominal breaths. This can slow our heart rate and help us think more clearly as well as assist in becoming more embodied. I believe this to be the first process for developing one's intuition. If we are deep in mind chatter and today's go-go-go existence, then we are surely not tapping into our intuitive abilities. To begin, dedicate three minutes in the morning hours and another three minutes in the evening hours to a conscious breathing practice. When we breathe consciously, we mentally follow the inhalations and exhalations, perhaps even with a focal point such as the nostrils. Notice the sensation at the nostrils. Can you feel the air pass through, moving in and out? If dedicating six minutes a day feels like too much to start, then take 30 seconds to breathe consciously each time you use the restroom, no matter where you are. No one will know. I always tell my clients that just about any restroom can act as a "private office" for grounding and breathing. It can be used as an escape whenever the need should arise—better that than to remain mentally scrambled, anxious, or what have you. In addition to breathing with awareness, use the sink as a grounding tool. Have you ever truly noticed the temperature of the water as it flows over the skin of your palms and fingers? How about the sensory difference between the parts of the hand that are the soapiest compared to the areas that are only wet with water? Placing our full attention on sensation is one way to ground. We can do this with sound as well. How many sounds can you detect in your environment right now?

Once we get comfortable with conscious breathing throughout the day and noticing our sensory experiences, we can begin to dedicate some time each day to sitting quietly and noticing what is taking place in our own physiology and nervous system. Is our heart rate and breathing regulated? Are there places of tension in our abdomen? What's going on in our mind? If we are overthinking, return to conscious breathing. With our newly developed breathing skills and attention placed on bodily sensation, we can lower our brain waves, move toward relaxation and go inward. This is a good time to do a body scan. To do this, turn your attention inward and mentally scan your body from the crown of the head to the soles of the feet. Move slowly and breathe. What do you notice? There might be places of discomfort or even extreme comfort. There may be places that feel warmer or cooler. An image may appear. Take this all in while continuing to just notice during your body scan. If emotions arise, allow them to. If it becomes too intense, stop there. Thank the body and know that you can do another scan at any time.

These are some ways to begin developing a relationship with ourselves. They slow us down, which is just what we need to develop intuition that is clean and clear. Intuition is connected to the body. All too often people confuse intuitive hits with information emerging from anxious states or old schemas and perceptions. With continued practice, we attune to our inner awareness more and more. Once body scans become familiar and comfortable, we can progress to dialoguing with whatever arises within us. For this, I suggest reclining in a comfortable chair or even lying down on a couch. Begin by breathing, as always, and you may even want to count down from ten to one. With each number, mentally state the intention to relax deeply and experience peace. This is one way to induce a mild level of self-hypnosis so that our faculties in this altered state can serve us well. From this place, I scan, notice, gather information, and bring loving healing energy where needed. When I feel complete, I like to count from one to ten with some energy behind it, while wiggling my fingers and toes. Taking notes of the experience is wise. I may do a grounding exercise and some stretching to come back into my body more fully before going on with the rest of my day.

This activity provides the relaxation that our nervous system and organs need in today's busy world. It also offers a platform for beginning to build a deeper relationship with the body, which is the place where so much information and wisdom is stored. Furthermore, our bodies cannot only be the conduit for intuiting with accuracy, but they can also be actually the source for healing. As we continue to develop and grow, the process becomes quicker and we can become the very vehicle of transformation.

The cover of the February 2020 issue of *Psychology Today* has one word in large font near the top: "Intuition." That issue is dedicated to the once again popular topic. It reads "Intuition: When to Trust Your Gut." The author, Matthew Hutson, lists "eight truths about intuition." I was pleased to see point number four which differentiates intuition from insight. Intuition is about the senses while insight is related to solution articulation, yet sometimes the two concepts are combined into one phenomenon. Snap judgments are also given attention and connect quick decision-making in a specific area (when there is no time for rational thought) with significant previous experience in that same area. Have you read Malcolm Gladwell's *Blink*? If so, you may recall the initial pages focusing on the kouros, which are archaic Greek statues of young men. Another kind of intuitive process is taking place there, like when you know something is wrong but can't say what it is.

Hutson reports how people are different; some are more intuitive than others. This difference can impact career, for instance. He uses the example of an accountant versus a counselor. Intuition may be supportive of those in the counseling field but not help someone in accounting. Some people, due to their jobs, may be able to develop intuition in different ways and at different rates. With all of these considerations, I suggest that through embodiment-focused daily practice, one can naturally develop intuitive processes that enhance day-to-day life as well as dreaming and other nonordinary states of consciousness. We can trust our intuition, I believe, given the right circumstances. What emerges from those states can have an impact on health and wellness—and that's what really matters here. The best time to begin is *now*. As you read further, you'll discover additional approaches to intuitive development that bring greater complexity.

When Jennifer Frank Tantia spoke at the Embodiment Conference in 2020, she explained how embodiment is both a state and a process. As a state, embodiment is inhabiting the body. "How do we cultivate embodiment? What does that process mean—what does it mean to become embodied or to cultivate your own embodiment through locating yourself or finding this sensory a static combination of embodied experience?" We have to slow down—thoughts are faster than the rhythm of the body. The process of embodiment is locating ourselves.

Considering the body as "a gateway between consciousness and unconsciousness, and when those two parts from our thoughts to our emotions to our embodied experience can speak to each other, we can start to find a more holistic way of living in ourselves," said Tantia. Interoceptive, kinesthetic, sensory and somatic nervous systems are involved here. There are more neurosynapses in our gut than in our brain! A description of embodiment by Eugene Gendlin can be thought of as a culmination of thought, sensation, posture, gesture and emotion (he brought us the technique called focusing). At this very moment, notice what your body is experiencing—that's embodiment. By taking in this information, we can understand why the notes in our dream journal do not necessarily need to be cognitive. All of our systems can inform us regarding the meaning or "take home message" of a dream. Instead, by recording a feeling or an emotion, a color, a felt sense, the experience we are having in our body at the moment we come out of a dream are all important information and I believe should be included in one's dream journal. I also suggest sketching the dream to reflect gesture and posture.

NINE

Italian Folkways

As noted earlier in this book, dreamwork, including the tracking of dreams, dream interpretation, and dream divination practices, have existed across time and place. Modern-day Italy is no exception. Even today, many Italian and Italian-American women (and some men) practice in the traditional way, which includes ideas and rituals surrounding dreams. Often, this "traditional way" is a complex combination of Catholic folk traditions mixed with traditional medicine and healing approaches. Sometimes, Catholicism is the "cover" for a more ancient tradition. Think of the archangel Saint Michael, Rosary beads, and a deck of prayer cards alongside garlic, salt, a corno (horn), ancestral artifacts, incantations, dream interpretation, and offerings to spirits of the home. As for dreams and omens, think of them as communication—it is the spirit world that initiates this contact and the dream space where most of this spirit communication and magic take place (Fahrun, 2018, p. 116). As suggested in earlier chapters, dream space exists outside of time and that liminal space between sleeping and waking states is precious. There, spiritual experiences can also occur whether it is contact with spirits or whether it is experiencing an unseen world.

In July 2019, I had the great pleasure to speak with Mary-Grace Fahrun of Rue's Kitchen. She likes to go by the name Grace. She is a healer in many regards: a registered nurse, expert practitioner of southern Italian women's traditional ways, and a Reiki master. Her book *Italian Folk Magic* is one of the greatest cultural treasures living on my bookshelf.

Grace heals with saint magic when called to do so. Not only does Grace use her Italian saint deck as an oracle, but she also has a working relationship with saints. Among Roman Catholics, saints were known to perform miracles (aka magic) during the time they were alive. Some claim that saints continue to perform their miracles through the living even today. Saints are associated with particular days of the year during which festivities are held to honor the saint's life. Anyone can begin to practice saint magic by first identifying the saint he or she feels closest to or the saint day his or her birthday falls on.

Having grown up Italian American in California and having attended eight years of Catholic school, I am quite familiar with the catechism of the Catholic Church. My father attended Catholic school for 12 years, was an altar boy for many of them, and studied Latin and Greco-Roman mythology, so the old gods and goddesses were not entirely unfamiliar. Since my father's confirmation in 1958, his favorite saint has been Saint Mark. He was blessed with a large extended family, which, unfortunately, means that I have been attending funerals since I was a very young child. Even though we have a hefty stack of prayer cards from those experiences, I was not explicitly taught saint magic (for those unfamiliar, prayer cards are like miniature postcards on card stock and sometimes laminated, with a colorful picture of a saint, the Virgin Mary, or Jesus Christ on one side and a corresponding prayer on the back side). Still, saints, guardian angels, and altars were important.

It is possible that one is introduced to a particular saint through a dream or vision, whether or not the dreamer is Catholic. During the time when I led a monthly dream group in the San Francisco Bay area, I met a woman who received an important message from a deity outside of the pantheon familiar to her in a vivid and profound dream, so stay open minded! From there, one may feel compelled to set up a shrine or home altar to that saint and make offerings (prayers, incense, candles, flowers, food). If this is new to you, don't be shy. See where this takes you—it is sure to develop. Remember, we must "feed" the energies we work with if we want to have a reciprocal relationship (more on this in the coming chapters). We can do this in the waking state, but also in the dream state. If you dream consciously, consider making an offering in that lucid dream space. You can do this shrine-making ritual for your ancestors in a similar fashion, as I'll describe later in this book.

Mary-Grace Fahrun and I agree that daydreams, visions and night dreams are all valuable, not just those dreams that occur during REM or deep sleep. In *Italian Folk Magic*, Grace explains how, with Italian folk dream interpretation, dreams of all kinds can be used to assess the effects of prayers as well as spell work. Dreams can even show an ill or afflicted person who cast the spell (*fattura*) or curse (*maledizione*) on him or her. A person's day-to-day subjective and objective symptoms can be interwoven with dreams, meaning that it is possible to detect the symptoms in the dream. After all, we are talking about the spectrum of consciousness here. While dreams are given attention in chapter eight, it is the ninth chapter of *Italian Folk Magic* which includes a specific list of dream images with their meanings. However, this is only the case for dreams where the dreamer is the observer, not the participant! The symbolic meanings can be used "to interpret the answer to your prayer or spell work" (Fahrun, 2018, p. 144). Grace told me that this list once belonged to her great aunt, who brought it with her from southern Italy. Its origins are believed to be from various towns and regions south of Rome and very old indeed.

During our conversation, Grace said, "So how this works is you cast a spell. Whenever there is magic involved in Italian witchcraft, the proof is in the dreaming afterwards. So how do you know if your spell worked? Well, the next day, when you wake up in the morning, or the middle of the night if it was so vivid that you woke up, you write down what you dreamt. Then you look up on the list to see whether your spell caught." She continued, "When I looked at this list, later on, with the knowledge of cartomancy and tarot, I understood that also the list requires interpretation based on the spell that you cast and then the dream that you have following." To be sure I understood, I offered a simple example. "So if you were doing some candle magic, for example, with a dressed green candle for increasing wealth, a prosperity spell, then that night you go to sleep and dream of someone smoking cigarettes." Grace affirmed my example and added, "Or bread. I have had the experience of doing a prosperity or money spell and dreaming of bread that night." So this is what this list is about (see the section on spells and charms in *Italian Folk Magic*). Whatever magic you're casting, if you dream of these things (referring to the contents of the list), "you can assess whether or not your spell worked." We talk about omens, premonitions, and precognitive dreams for a bit, then I ask about the observer-participant distinction. Again, Grace highlighted that our discussion was strictly about experiences for when the dreamer is the observer; "that's what's specific about these, and only the observer." When the dreamer is an active participant in the dream scenario, it's completely different. For these cases, dream interpretation revolves around what is going on in the dreamer's life. It's "basically like a tarot card reading."

Grace reflected on Italian dream culture experienced in her childhood and shared some of the means of diagnosis carried out by her family members. "Suppose I've been sad or depressed or whatever. The typical check up, every day, from an Italian relative, would be 'Did you eat today?' 'Did you dream last night?' Usually it was 'What did you dream last night?' This was to assess your state of mind and whether there was sorcery involved." This naturally leads to debating the dream interpretations of snakes and serpents. This is important for me personally, since I dream and journey with snakes often, yet according to this southern Italian list, there is an unfavorable connection to dreams with snakes (Fahrun, 2018). I point out the ancient historical admiration, respect, and blessings of dream snakes and serpents, as they have long been connected to transformation, power, healing, primal energy, and life force. I even shared with Grace a few photos of ancient Greek artifacts (from the Archeological Museum of Thessaloniki) depicting snakes casted with gold becoming beautiful jewelry for the living and the dead. Evidence can also be found in burial sites along with skeletal remains. Grace told me how some people believe what is in the book or list and how some of her personal beliefs and practices differ. She thinks it is important to notice how the dreamer feels about the dream and how one feels when waking up. Personal life experiences impact these things, as well as centuries of religious influence, so there is much to consider here. We exchanged stories that support this outlook. "In parts of Southern Italy, like Napoli, the snake is venerated," Grace told me. "The snake is rebirth. The snake is transformation." We discuss the snake procession, *la festa dei serpari*, that still takes place in Abruzzo. In the end, there can be so many vantage points, so many interpretations. This is especially true of the image of the serpent, given its extensive history.

I was thrilled to hear Grace claim, "Dream interpretation is something that, I feel, people should be doing every day. I think it should be part of someone's spiritual practice, even their mental health practice." She laughed. "Look who I'm talking to!" When a client in a heightened emotional state comes to see Grace, she hears herself asking the same questions as her aunts and the previous generations once asked: "How are you sleeping? What are you dreaming? Are these dreams in the middle of the night? Are these dreams waking you up?" She shared some important distinctions with me: "If you are dreaming something as you are waking up, then that is a message that is pertinent. Whichever spirit or whichever mechanism that is sending you that message, well, it is something that is pertinent to the immediate future! Whereas dreams that occur in the middle of the night, and you kind of wake up haunted, but cannot grasp, are not premonitions, but it is a warning system, like an orange light alerting you that there is something in your periphery to be aware of. Now, recurrent dreams.... I love recurrent dreams."

The conversation turned toward me, and I told her of my recurring dreams of serpents. I even shared with her some of my dream-inspired art works, as several paintings, pastel drawings, and collages were next to me, all depicting snakes. Grace has a fear of snakes in everyday life, unlike me; however, she feels differently about snakes that appear in her dreams. These details should be considered when interpreting dreams. As we practice this ancient art and hone our skills, it is sure to carry us along our path, supporting our unique journeys.

Now for some more fun! *La Smorfia Napoletana*, a type of dream dictionary from Napoli, contains a list of numbers with the associated words (evoking images), strictly for predicting lottery numbers. Here are four examples, taken from the website www.

lasmorfianapoletana.com (see the classic smorfia list) and the book *Italian Folk Magic* (Fahrun, 2018):

13 Sant' Antonio (Saint Anthony)
48 'O Muorto che pparla (a dead person that speaks)
61 'O Cacciatore (an armed hunter)
81 'E Sciure (a field of flowers)

This system is believed to assist those who want to win the lottery (as long as he or she keeps quiet about it)—it's serious business. Would you like to try this method for yourself? In the morning, write down your dream immediately. Reflect on the dream imagery, which should correspond to one or more particular numbers. The numbers, in some combination, are expected to be the lottery's winning numbers. *Buona fortuna!*

TEN

Surprise Visitors

P EOPLE OFTEN RECALL DREAM IMAGES of other people, yet sometimes these *others* can be surprising. Across time and place, people report dreaming with babies-to-be, the deceased, and even older children that may want our attention.

Announcing Dreams

Pregnancy folklore is rich, culturally and personally. In my 2018 book *Extraordinary Dreams: Visions, Announcements and Premonitions Across Time and Place*, you will find a section titled "Fetal Sex Predictions" in chapter three. There, I shared a story my mother recalled. Among those in her inner circle, one's wedding ring and a string were used for foretelling the sex of the baby. That sounds like a homemade pendulum, I thought. This method is only one of many that are used to forecast fetal sex. According to one study, relying on dreams or feelings to predicts fetal sex is more reliable than folkloric methods (Perry, DiPietro, & Costigan, 1999). Let me tell you about a dream that one woman shared with me. It contains two predictive elements:

> *An adult-size baby boy ... was leaning on my bed, watching my husband and I sleeping. When I got up to look at him, he calmly whispered, "I'm coming."*

A month later, to her great satisfaction, the dreamer conceived her first child, after months of attempting to get pregnant. This is one example of an announcing dream, one that "freaked out" the dreamer but also served as a prediction for what was to come.

Fascinating dream visions date back to ancient times. These include big announcements or announcing dreams. One example found in the King James version of the Bible (see Matthew 1:20) is the announcement of the conception of Jesus: "But while he thought on these things, behold, the angel of the Lord appeared unto him in a dream, saying, Joseph, thou son of David, fear not to take unto thee Mary thy wife: for that which is conceived in her is of the Holy Ghost."

In another example from the Bible (see Luke 1:13–15), an angel announces the future birth of John the Baptist to his father. "Fear not, Zacharias, for thy prayer is heard, and thy wife Elizabeth shall bear thee a son, and thou shalt call his name John. And thou shalt have joy and gladness, and many shall rejoice at his birth. For he shall be great in the sight of the Lord, and shall drink neither wine nor strong drink, and he shall be filled with the Holy Ghost even from his mother's womb."

Dreams can be a powerful healing force during life's big transitional periods, such as conception, pregnancy or birth, marriage, children leaving the home, retirement, and death. In fact, meaningful and memorable dreams are often reported during these times in people's lives. They can assist psychological adjustment and even with the grief process. Contemporary Westerners, many of them Christian, just don't talk about dreams much. For whatever reason, dreaming seems to have been cast out, along with experiencing visions and other intuitive ways of knowing, into a realm of superstition or faulty beliefs. It seems a little strange given that the New Testament includes them. It is not this way in much of the rest of the world, however. In Islam, for instance, dreams hold status and are taken seriously—they play a role in everyday life affairs and carry a high level of authority. For example, a dream can influence who and when one should marry. Dreams may be consulted regarding big business decisions. In a way, you could say that some dreams are prophecy, given all we know about them. I have read that some of the Qur'an was given to Muhammad in dreams, yet others claim that the Qur'an was given to Muhammad directly by Allah. Basically, dreams are included in the holy books of the world's major religions.

Thinking about life transitions again, it must be noted that dreams also bring healing and comfort to those approaching the most profound transition of all, death. As also mentioned, dreams, too, can support families prior to pregnancy or the time of birth. These transitional times are impactful in the lives of so many. In my book *Extraordinary Dreams: Visions, Announcements, and Premonitions Across Time and Place*, I dedicate a significant amount of space to the phenomena of announcing dreams. You may have heard the terms "conception dream" or "fertility dream." Like conception or fertility dreams, announcing dreams are most often experienced by a parent (usually it is the mother) near conception or during pregnancy. An announcing dream goes a bit further in that it also includes visual, tactile, or auditory pre-birth communication in which the unborn child makes an appearance in some way, so that the dreamer perceives an experience of genuine communication. These experiences are often moving and go well beyond a fantasy-like dream of a baby. Predictions are cast, names are foretold, and fetal sex is revealed.

It is likely no surprise that announcing dreams, even just one, appear to enhance prenatal bonding. Dozens of women I spoke with told me that they felt closer to the baby they were carrying after a memorable announcing dream, regardless of how specific or detailed it had been. Some of the dreams involved the dreaming mother caring for a baby or playing with a young child. When the dreamer awoke, she felt certainty regarding the fetal sex. This brought with it excitement. For those that feel fearful over what is to come, such as some first-time mothers, announcing dreams can soothe worries and fears.

One pregnant woman said, "I'm just holding her, taking her some place with me. The common themes in all the dreams is a great love and connection toward her." There was "a sense of anxiety about not being able to financially provide," possibly from "my own material related to my past as a child and also deep fears I have presently even before getting pregnant" (Mascaro, 2018). Announcing dreams support a pregnant woman's mental health and wellness. For many, fear transforms into a sense of calmness and anxiety into peace.

Some announcing dreams provide information that can be

helpful to a wide range of healthcare providers, including grief counselors, doulas and midwives. I know someone who dreamed that her fully developed baby was breech, which gave time to consider options and treatments. Another woman I know had a powerful vivid dream shortly after conception but before the miscarriage, where the dream infant told her that it didn't belong to her, stating, "I'm not your baby" (Mascaro, 2018). Other announcing dreams influence the decisions pregnant women make regarding prenatal care or the decision to terminate the pregnancy. One woman I knew had a meaningful out-of-body experience with her fetus, which led to declining the recommended amniocentesis. A few women told me they canceled an abortion appointment, because despite severe hardship, the dream showed them that a positive, stable future for them and their child was possible. In some of those cases, the pregnant dreamer was lucid and engaged in dialogue, played games, or did other caring actions with their dream baby. Dreams and other meaningful experiences emerging from nonordinary states of consciousness can support as well as provide insight into women's reproductive health choices. Dreams are our helpers, showing up in service. Furthermore, announcing dreams and visitation dreams sit well together. These two categories of dreams are like bookends. Announcing dreams open a portal for how life on earth begins and where it can lead, while visitation dreams show us how earthly life ends and the mysteries that await us. If you are wondering, "Well, can't a dream visit from the yet-to-be-born be considered a visitation dream?" My response would be "Sure it can." However, for the sake of discussion and to reduce unnecessary confusion, let's compartmentalize these two phenomena for now. Birth and death are part of a natural cycle of wholeness and offer powerful opportunities for healing, regardless of how we label them. In the next section, we examine visitations.

Disembodied Visitors and Visitation Dreams

As I exit the building, I notice how it is such a warm and sunny day. I see my beloved Nonni sitting on a structure, like a cement block, in a park.

She is having a lively conversation on a cell phone (even though they were not common when she was living). "How strange," I think. I have a good feeling when I see her. She's wearing a pretty violet and blue dress.... As I greet her with a touch and a kiss, I can feel and I can smell her [taken from a segment of a dream logged in my dream journal in April 2020].

Across time and place, discarnate souls, deceased family or community members, and the like have made themselves known to dreamers. For those who are bereaved dreaming of the deceased is remarkably common and most often a positive experience among those with a high level of dream recall (Black et al., 2019). As you read ahead, please understand that not all dreams of this type will be uplifting and nightmares are possible (Foor, 2017).

Sometimes, the discarnate are not known to the dreamer and are only identified as divine beings or as gods or goddesses from a forgotten past. There are numerous reports of advice, consolation, direct instructions, and warnings given to the living by the dead in the dream or vision state. When the dreamer experiences such, we call these visitation dreams because they are said to feel like an actual visit. Visitation dreams are typically highly sensorial, vivid and vibrant. I'll share with you another especially vivid and impactful visitation that occurred just over a decade ago. This dream featured a neighbor who had recently died. Everyone in our courtyard referred to him as "Chief" because he watched over the community.

It's a bright, sunny day. My bedroom window is open wide. I'm sitting on my bed, looking out the window facing the community courtyard fountain. Everything is vibrant and colorful. Chief walks toward me without his cane and appears more youthful than usual. I know he had died recently, but that was not a concern. Chief is able to come right up to the edge of my bedroom window since the large green bush that exists in front of the window in physical waking reality is not there in the dream. This allows me to climb halfway out and sit on the windowsill as we greet each other. Our interaction is warm and pleasant. Briefly, we communicate, but without words. He looks really good—healthy, full of life and also peaceful.

That day, I felt touched and was really glad to have had the chance to "see" him again. Visitation dreams are often quite memorable and meaningful; they can be this way even for those in our life outside of family.

A client who came to see me in my private practice reported frequent visitation dreams over an eight- to nine-year period after the death of her parent by suicide. Some of the dreams came with a wide range of feelings while other times there was a sense of neutrality. She claimed that the visitation dreams could be helpful in understanding her feelings about the tragic ordeal as well as a way to get a glimpse of what was taking place on the other side. Another came to similar conclusions after years of sporadically recalled dreams of her deceased brother. She felt he was communicating with and watching over her.

Dreams are associated with the spirit world in many cultures past and present, such as Roman, Celt, ancient Greek, Egyptian, Muslim, ancient Hebrew, Persian, some Christian, and even the Bahá'í faith (Krippner et al., 2002). Sleeping on the grave or tomb of a relative or ancestor is an old tradition. Based on accounts of early Irish history and ritual, an "inspired" Celt might consume raw animal flesh and blood and sleep in its hide to wake up with insight, direct advice or instruction regarding a challenging situation.

On the path to becoming a shaman, one's deceased family members teach special songs, in dreams, imbued with magical powers, for the South American Guarani. Whether dreaming or awake, seeing spirits "is the determining sign of the shamanic vocation ... having contact with the souls of the dead signifies being dead oneself" (Eliade, 2004, p. 84).

Disembodied entities unknown to the dreamer have warned people of developing diseases in their bodies. Kathleen O'Keefe-Kanavos describes her experiences in the book *Dreams That Can Save Your Life*, as mentioned earlier, but also in even greater depth in her 2014 book *Surviving Cancerland: Intuitive Aspects of Healing*. In Kathleen's case, a figure that looked like a monk came into her dreams on multiple occasions to give news, direction and instruction, ultimately saving her life. During a phone conversation we had in the spring of 2020, Kathleen told me, "The monks were with me for all three cancers. They were with me every step of the way." In

Surviving Cancerland, these dreams and others guided her through five years' worth of treatments. I thought about how our spirit guides, whether angels or animals or something else, come through to help us when we need help the most. Kathleen added, "Our spirit guides pick us—we don't pick them." I wholeheartedly agreed. Sometimes they appear as the last thing we would expect. If we don't pay attention or remain open, our guides may appear in dreams in an extravagant way or may behave wildly. Kathleen's guides came in dreams and literally screamed at her, for her health was again in jeopardy. Furthermore, she experienced recurrent dreams which were both precognitive and diagnostic in nature because they were experienced *before* the conventional pathology reports confirmed the breast cancer diagnosis thus giving validation to the dreams. The take home point for me, in my own healing journey, is that I should remain open to all forms of intuitive guidance and not judge the incoming guidance based on expectations.

An Indigenous American woman who attended one of my dream groups some years ago said that a goddess from the Hindu pantheon appeared to her in a dream conveying an important message. The dreamer was shocked not only by the message but by the fact that a figure completely unfamiliar in her world would make a connection in this way. In this particular case, the healing aspect was more of an emotional one, which helped her integrate and later accept a previously challenging and difficult situation.

During my time as a trauma psychotherapist at a nonprofit agency in California, women would report deceased friends or family appearing in dreams. One Puerto Rican woman reported frequent recurring dreams with her beloved deceased sister. This client felt that her relationship with her deceased sister could continue as long as the dreams did. She felt mostly comforted by these experiences, which prompted dialogue and positive action around her recovery from substance abuse. As part of motivational interviewing, the imagined opinions of the client's deceased sister came into play. What would my dead sister expect of me, hope for me, need from me? How can my best life also honor my sister and her memory? This exploration, fueled through visitation dreams, supported the client's recovery process. During our time together, I invited my client to participate in an expressive creative project I have used with myself as well as other clients—altar-making, or the construction of a small shrine. As dreams themselves may bring healing, what better way to honor the dream and the deceased who visit us through them? Shrine-making was comfortable for her—nothing new for this Catholic client. The finished product can be used as a sacred space for prayer at home and for making offerings to the dead. This altar allowed the client to give tokens of appreciation to her sister that could now only visit in the dream space. These actions enhanced as well as deepened the relationship with and connection to her sister on "the other side of the veil."

At the 2019 Ashland, Oregon, regional conference of the IASD, I gave an art workshop. This workshop intersected visitation dreams of deceased loved ones with altar-making. I was touched by each participant's beautifully adorned wooden shrines, dedicated to a lost loved one. One female veteran attended the workshop and shared her story involving two tours in Afghanistan alongside her fellow military service people. One man in particular was a close friend who sadly, after returning home, completed suicide. As a way to honor him, the dreams, and the friendship that blossomed between them as military veterans surviving alongside one another, she created a shrine for him. I do not know how the visitation dreams may have developed or shifted after the workshop, but I do know that this action was a meaningful response to all that took place between them.

In some of these cases, the dream experience is one directional, meaning that the dream pops up, an action is made, and that is it. Other times, it is more of a dual-directional, multi-layered experience. When this is the case, a dream may occur, then the dreamer completes some action. From there, another dream may occur. In Kathleen's case, she at first did not act on the information given in the dream, so another dream followed before she took action. In my client's case, she eventually made an offering (crafting the altar) in response to the dreams. Basically, the daytime action taken by these two women then led to another dream and then another. I think of this kind of back-and-forth behavior as a call-and-response. I believe spirit pays attention. This is not mediumship, nor is it channeling. The deceased does not communicate through the mouth or body as is commonly done among Spiritualists. Instead, what develops is a relationship fostered by the healing aspects of the dream, what I call dream medicine. Dream medicine can be practiced abundantly, in 101 variations. As long as our access to that imaginal space where dreams and visions unfold is not severed, and serves emotional, physical, spiritual or mental healing, we are on the right track.

In his book *The Dreamer's Book of the Dead*, Robert Moss discusses why the dead come calling in the first place. Moss finds that the deceased visit for many of the same reasons the living visit each other: to make amends, to deal with unfinished business, to give counsel or express love, to provide information (which can sometimes be unreliable) about current or future events, or to perform other actions. With this in mind, I ponder a dream from January 2021 in which I have a procedure followed by an outdoor gathering. Many family members gather (both deceased and living) to tell me that I will be receiving a reward. In the dream I ask, "A reward for what?" I express how I'm doing all right and already feel rewarded in life, yet they claim that a much bigger reward is coming. I continue to wonder what exactly am I being rewarded for and how this reward will show up in my life. A few days later, I opened an email to learn that my manuscript would soon be published, turning into this book you are reading now. Exciting as this was, in the back of my mind I recalled an approaching medical appointment for another MRI. Would my reward be related to my health concerns? Only time will tell.

Could the dead also appear in dreams and visions to show us that consciousness exists beyond the physical body? Moss thinks so. He writes, "Our dead may come to us to make us aware that the soul has a life beyond the body. They may come to help us get ready for our own journeys beyond death. Sometimes they take us on tours of afterlife locales through which we can develop interesting connections and study the real estate options on the Other Side" (Moss, 2005, p. 45). For those grieving the loss of a loved one or for those in the dying process themselves, visitation dreams are like medicine.

As a lifelong dreamer, psychologist Enjolie Lafaurie told me about how she views and experiences dreams. "When I dream, I pay special attention to the feeling of the dream. I dream vividly, in detail, and in color. Sometimes I take my dreams to therapists or friends to process them. While some of my dreams are stress-related, many more are visitations. I experience a lot of visitation dreams. My dreams reflect synchronicity and also offer affirmation and confirmation. Dreams can confirm waking reality in practical ways, and can reflect who we truly are in conjunction with our current struggles. They can act as a guide concerning daily situations."

Blending Western psychology with her Indigenous spirituality, Lafaurie looks at dreams from two angles. Sometimes her dreams provide insight from the context of her independent, individual self, while other times her dreams mirror an interdependent reality without boundaries. Why wouldn't the energies of others we are close to merge with our own energies when we dream? Language also comes into play here. The way we speak about dreaming differs among languages and reflects our beliefs about the phenomenon. We compare Spanish and English phrases, such as to "dream with" ("sueño con") as compared to "dream of." The belief system is reflected in the language itself. Dreaming is not a passive process.

Lafaurie and I found a common interest in the phenomena of visitation dreams and the real connection that unfolds from those experiences. Lafaurie told me about her interest in the afterlife since her childhood. She stated, "Dreams are not time-bound or linear. We must let the dream evolve, just as we would allow a prayer to evolve. We shouldn't expect a quick fix or immediate resolution. As mindfulness practices teach us, we must sit with the discomfort for a while."

"In my family," Lafaurie shared, "we expect a visitation dream when someone passes away. We even ask each other if a visitation has taken place. It is so ingrained in us that if someone does not receive one soon after a death, that person can feel bad or ashamed." As we continued talking, Lafaurie recalled visitation dreams from several family members after their deaths, including her husband

and father who both died from cancer a day apart, and years later, her cousin who died by suicide. Her relationship with her late husband and father continues through dreams. For Lafaurie, "the quality of each of these visitation dreams differs depending on many things: what was taking place in the life of the person along with the context of their passing, in addition to their personality, relational and unresolved issues. The walk they have in the physical world informs the walk they have in the spirit world. The dream is just another medium or format to continue developing the relationship and working through our issues."

Just one visitation dream can spark emotional healing for those on their deathbed as well as those experiencing the deep pain that comes with losing a loved one. During her time working with people facing life-threatening illness as a hospice social worker and bereavement counselor, Jeanne Van Bronkhorst saw more than most do. She writes that "visitation dream visitors wait with the dying person and provide comfort just with their presence. They welcome, they smile, and they wait patiently," bringing about a profound calmness and sense of peace. "Their presence alone lessens anxiety and pain in the dreamers" (Van Bronkhorst, 2015, p. 85). Even when medical professionals cannot save an ill person from an approaching death, encouraging dialogue or relationships with dream visitors, instead of dismissing them as hallucinations or delusions, can initiate mental and emotional healing. For those still living and grieving the loss of a loved one, a visitation dream can be a catalyst for healing old wounds.

The many visitation dreams I have experienced have included paternal family members. Each experience has reminded me that family bonds continue post-death and have helped ease the emotional pain and maladaptive thinking that can come along with sudden or even multiple deaths of loved ones. I notice similar outcomes with my clients, especially those that have lost family, friends, or significant others from disease, including addiction. Instead of fueling old beliefs like "building relationships is pointless because they won't last," healthier patterns can bloom ("I know she is proud of me and wants me to do well because she brought that rose to my workplace in last night's dream"). For these cognitive and emotional shifts alone, I believe that bringing dreams into any health practice is of value.

When one shares a visitation dream with a group of grieving individuals, such as their family, a great shift may occur. A dream recalled by one member can be a gift for the entire group that aids in coping and confirmation of the existence of an afterlife. Visitation dreams support a healthy mourning process for many people.

Sometimes we might dream of a deceased celebrity, even one only vaguely familiar. These kinds of visitation dreams invoke mystery. About three weeks after the death of celebrity chef Anthony Bourdain, I had a surprising dream.

I'm with a guy, perhaps a boyfriend. We are picking up tickets for a motel or a place to sleep. I'm not sure why we need to stay there. The guy gets his ticket and walks off. Inside a building, I enter a particular room to get mine. Then, I notice Anthony Bourdain—he is there off in the distance talking to people. It seems to be a book event. This particular room is large with a dining area in the back. Even though I am a dollar short, the salesperson sells me a copy of his book. I go to order some food even though I don't know how I will pay for it. I finally open the book and see that it's a signed copy! As the evening progresses, I see people mill about and leave. I'm sitting at a little round table in the back, alone. Anthony Bourdain approaches and sits down at my table. We just start talking about normal stuff—food, travel. As the conversation continues, he realizes I am from the San Francisco Bay area so he comments on a pizza joint in the area. I say, "Nothing compares to pizza in Napoli." He smiles and I add, "You know what I'm talking about" because I know how much he has traveled and that he knows from where specific foods originate. I tell him I've traveled a bit and that I have family from Italy. I tell him about Bagna Calda (a garlic dish from the Piedmonte region of Northern Italy) and say, "Funny—no matter which restaurant I go to, no one makes it the way it's made at home, or the way the family does," knowing he will appreciate that comment. He seems to take this in as we talk and laugh about how "home-style" just can't be replicated. It seems like I've been there for quite a while—I think we eat pizza together. I get a sense that it is time to go. I'm now even more lucid. I know he is dead and I figure that he knows it too. So I say, "Hey, man, I'm so sorry about what happened. It's really sad [in reference to his death]. I hope you're going to be okay." He just nods while looking downward with a faint smile. It feels like an acknowledgment yet I perceive him as feeling bad about it all. We sit in silence. I think that it's weird to say what I said but I feel I had to acknowledge the accusation of his suicide. At this point the guy from earlier returns. The dream ends.

I have never read one of Bourdain's books; I never followed him in his early career. Yet near the end of his life, I began to notice him and appreciate his show *Parts Unknown*. This was not my last dream with Bourdain, but the first. His presence in my dreams has surprised me and I still do not understand why he has made appearances. The deceased can pop in regardless of our history with them and can leave us with mixed emotions, among them confusion. While I do not have a history of celebrity dreams, perhaps I had something unresolved surrounding his death. In the imaginal realm, anything is possible. Sometimes we sit with the dead in order to get well.

The variety of topics in this book hold great meaning in my life, but this particular topic is high on the list. For more stories and dreams regarding visitations, see my 2018 book *Extraordinary Dreams: Visions, Announcements and Premonitions Across Time and Place*. There, I share more of my own as well as those of others I interviewed.

Along the Recovery Road

There is so much wisdom in dreams. Whether addiction is a disease of the brain, the spirit, or both is yet to be determined conclusively. Over the years, I have learned a great deal about what it means to share dreams and how dreams pop up in unexpected times in order to be a source of support and guidance to those living with addiction. I'll share a couple of memories with you here.

When walking the road of recovery and working to overcome addiction, dreams often surface. When my psychotherapy clients would speak of them, Jeremy Taylor, D. Min., would come to mind. Jeremy worked with dreams for over 50 years and authored the 1983 classic *Dream Work: Techniques for Discovering the Creative Power in Dreams*. He was known for saying that "dreams come in service of health and wholeness" (I can still hear his voice), and only the dreamer can say for certain what her dreams mean.

After a few months of "clean time," my clients would report a dream or a series of dreams depicting the drug of choice. Several women told me similar stories of how, in the dream, they would just look at a pipe, a bag of meth, or a crack rock sitting on a table or in the palm of a hand, yet they would not move toward it or try to obtain it. Similarly, some clients would hold or fiddle with the drug in the dream but not ingest it. Upon awakening, they reported pounding hearts, perspiration, intense fear or feelings of dread, and at the same time, a commitment to recovery was re-established. This is sensitive territory. After a period of clean time, many have had a slip, thereby "picking up" again, which can lead to an overdose.

"I'll never go back," one young woman claimed. "I just can't live like that anymore," said another. "I'm too scared to relapse," piggy-backed a middle-aged woman. Statements like these were produced after a dream was shared in group or individual sessions. These dreams may have come just in time, as a way to remind the client that her old life was not working for her. Such dreams may serve to warn. One's concerns are reflected in dreams, reminding the person with addiction that danger lurks around every corner and how easy it is to slip. As noted above slipping can lead to death. Our consciousness, the higher self, is oriented toward evolution: wholeness and health. The medicine of dreams can act as a guiding compass of healing, pointing north, toward the heavens.

Sometimes for the addicted person, the child-self appears in a dream. I have suggested to some of my clients that instead of fearing or running from the child to make an alliance. It is often the case that substance-abusing women have survived several threats to life and personal violations since early childhood (physical and sexual assault, severe neglect, recurring childhood molestation), as far back as they can mentally recall, and sometimes even as far back as their bodies remember. I would ask them to imagine what this dream child might need and how we might be able to make her an offering, thus building an alliance. If the client preferred to send the dream child away, I've suggested that we give her something she might need in her journey alone—a power object or tool of some sort. By using guided imagery to guide clients into the imaginal realm, followed by creative and expressive art, I found that these experiences would help open the doorway to their own internal medicine, long dormant in their hearts. Sometimes the offering would be collaborative; I had been invited to honor the young wounded survivor, while other times I sat back to hold space and witness transformation begin.

This work can be done effectively without any mention of metaphysical or spiritual belief systems. We can call it *working with the imagination*, if that suits a client more. What we call or label these types of experiences is not important. Furthermore, I do not tell my clients that time is illusory and that past, present and future are all taking place *now*. There is no need for that. What matters most is that there is an intuitive knowing or felt sense—a shift which brings them more deeply into the heart, connecting to the wisdom of their body and breath, an emotional experience of reconnecting to their higher purpose, and remembering who they truly are. When it comes to working with dreams, it is not the diagnosis that is of interest either, but the way in which professionals or group members hold space for the dreamer. Please remember, before and after this kind of work, it is important to ground yourself and the client. To close, let me reiterate, there is wisdom in dreams.

ELEVEN

Animal and Plant
Spirit Guidance

IN 1986, THE READER'S DIGEST ASSOCIATION published a book titled *Magic and Medicine of Plants*. The editors of the book included an introduction which reminds the readers that plants have helped humankind across the world "from time immemorial" and that about half of all prescribed medicines are derived from plants (p. 5). When it comes to the sacred, magical or supernatural, some plants hold special status even today. Vervain and garlic appear among the top contenders, having held on to their positive status since ancient times in the Mediterranean, while belladonna (and others of the nightshade family) has been associated with the wicked due to its potentially deadly effects. Another Mediterranean plant, the mandrake, stands in both worlds—of veneration and of evil. In that same region, trees and flowers were associated with specific gods and goddesses—each viewed as a living link to the respective deity. Tree resin (amber) was even believed to be the tears shed by the daughters of the sun. Moving further north, mistletoe claims a high status. It lives between earth and sky, never having emerged from the ground as all other plants do. Mistletoe is said to hold both sacred and healing properties. *Magic and Medicine of Plants* also describes the Christianization of once-pagan plants in Europe and the impact of Christianization on the Aztec population once the conquistadors witnessed the Aztecs' relationships with local plants. Even through religious oppression, people have maintained their relations with the plant kingdom. Some even took them back later.

The notion of spirit entities embodying the natural world (animism) is a human tendency. It is also a feature of shamanism.

Totemism, which is related to shamanism, is a "spiritual or psychological connection of human beings with the natural world, such as animals, plants, or any other objects around human beings"—both are seemingly connected with Eastern beliefs and Native American spirituality (Lee & Kanazawa, 2015, p. 265). In applying some aspect of nature to a group's identity, totemism exists as an important process connecting an animal species with a group's ancestors and deities, thus ensuring the totem's well-being through ceremonies and special rites. These spirit guardian relations directly affect members of the group (Winkelman, 2015).

Today, in the contemporary West, totem relations exist yet they may not be acknowledged or understood so easily or carry the same level of meaning as in the distant past. Still, many people report a totem revealing itself again and again. In my dreaming, Anaconda appeared frequently over a period of a few years. Here is the third in a series of anaconda dreams.

I'm in an archaic bathhouse—it feels like something from ancient Mediterranean times with tall, bone-white columns. I'm clothed and standing on the edge, only observing. The water is shallow and murky in some places. I know that an anaconda is there. A female figure is standing next to me. I think it is my mother. I suggest that she remain alert while pointing to the anaconda underneath the surface of the water, as it is consuming a human. I say, "You see, it just killed a man." I walk away from her and the spot where I had been standing. Slowly making my way towards the right, along the edge as to not get wet, the anaconda begins to emerge from the water right in front of me. With the lower half of its body still submerged, it raises its head and we are eye to eye. We remain there gazing at each other. I realize that this could be the end of me, so I slowly, very slowly, move away. The anaconda follows but I do not rush. The scene fades and I wake up in bed.

The creation story of the Abenaki (an indigenous population originally of the northeastern United States) teaches us not to question our dreams, as Great Spirit dreamed us into existence. What Great Spirit dreamed came true. Dreams are our creation, literally. This is also the case for the entire plant and animal kingdom. We all come from the same place ... the dream. Without dreaming, would we even exist?

Here, I will share a little more about shamanism in relation to this topic of spiritual guidance. For animals that offer spiritual help and service to the shaman, their characteristics, powers, and traits may be gained. We may recall aspects of shamanism involving animals: "the shaman was believed to be killed by animals in a death-and-rebirth initiatory experience, the shaman's power was derived from animals, the shaman was believed to be able to transform into an animal, the shaman enacted animal behaviors and sounds in rituals," and the shaman was believed to be able to control animals, bringing them to waiting hunters (Winkelman, 2015, p. 273).

On shamanic journeys, through drumming, dreaming, or other activities, a shaman becomes the power animal in order to be helped with the journey's mission. This identity and integration takes place through the "visionary state of consciousness" (Cowan, 1993, p. 151). Similarly, healing witches, or wise women, also had a relationship with animal helpers in both waking and dream states. I must highlight one point here! When I use the term "witch," I am referring to a traditional European healer, magician, seer, or prophet, who (most often a woman) was directly targeted during the times of the Inquisition along with its outreaching tentacles we see even today. I am also including a large range of groups here, whether they are of Celt, Germanic, Mediterranean, or Nordic origin or whether they existed as gifted in certain domains such as midwifery or herbalism. Going back as far as the Classical times, witches have been associated with herbs, flowers, and plants (Grimassi, 2007). The modern English word pharmacy is derived from ancient Greek words connected to witches, spells, and herbalism. This can be a very sensitive topic for some people, so allow me to offer clarification. When I say "witch" or "witchcraft" I am not talking about the descriptions from witch-hunters during the burning times or the institution of the Church, which saw these wise women (and sometimes men) as sole practitioners of evil that set out to make pacts with the devil or cause harm to others. These accusations were unfounded. Much of the witch craze developed out of control and dominance politically and financially. When I use the term witch or speak of the craft, I am talking about something much bigger, a practice or way of becoming whole. In my book (no pun intended), witches are just like anyone else, except that they have gained an intimate knowledge of the natural and spiritual worlds as well as unseen forces such as elemental powers. Witches are connected with Mother Earth, her offspring, and celestial forces. The people who practiced these traditional ways gave aid to those in childbirth and in illness and pain. The earliest examples of medicine were birthed through these folkways.

Other cultures might use the term "witch" to mean something entirely different, so always use caution and ask questions when this term comes up in discussion or writings. The response will come from one's historical and cultural point of view. Some of the common animals that witches or traditional practitioners had a magical relationship or a soul connection with included cats, owls, ducks, geese, goats, pigs, wolves, hare, ravens, crows, lizards, bats, and likely several more. These animals were referred to as "familiars." Leviticus 20:27 in the Old Testament states that death by stoning is the appropriate response for those that have a familiar spirit or consult with spirits, for these are capital offenses. This is again referenced later in the first book of Samuel. During Europe's Dark Ages especially, these animals were blamed for doing the work of the witch in order to conceal her, or sometimes his, identity. As noted above, witches were believed to be able to turn themselves into animals. In the early 1700s in Hungary, those accused "exhibited remarkable shamanic features, including fertility battles and shapeshifting rituals" (Cowan, 1993, p. 152). Tests and initiation are also similar to others found throughout shamanism, in this case, experiencing dismemberment during three-day trance states.

Ambar Past (2005) wove together a unique book reflecting ways of living and healing of the Maya, *Incantations: Songs, Spells, and Images by Mayan Women*. This book taught me about tragic events that took place on their land as a result of invasion, colonization and religious persecution. In the 16th century, Friar Diego de Landa (in his Relacion de las cosas de Yucatan) noted the exquisite beauty of Mayan books along with the great sadness of the Mayan people as Franciscan friars burned them. Only four pre–Columbian Mayan books survived. Mayan classical literature was close to being completely wiped out as a result of the invasion. Today, however, books live in the hearts of the wise Maya. A song cannot be burned. Learning this, I reflected on other societies and cultures that have suffered colonization. Have oral traditions remained strong because of these histories, out of necessity? I don't know, but whether or not that's the case, song, sound and poetry are gifts from the spirit world. They are used to heal and maintain health for the community in shamanic societies all over the world.

The Tzotzil-speaking Maya acknowledge illness as a result of soul loss. Loss can happen as a result of injury, fear, or theft (by those who inflict harm). This is not just a physical human concern as illnesses may arise when the soul of one's *wayhel* (animal companion) is lost, injured, or captured, for example. When wayhel souls run about during dreaming all sorts of things can happen. When wayhel get sick, so do their owners. Those who cure such ailments are taught to do so in dreams. The songs and incantations come from that place, a gift of the ancestors, the First Fathermothers, keepers of the Great Book.

Many spiritual traditions, traditional belief systems and cultures, including creation myths, embrace the notion of spirit helpers. These helpers can appear in animal or plant form, often in a dream or vision or trance state. Norse mythology, Germanic paganism, stregheria, Mayan traditional ways, and some of the North American First Nations creation stories and legends are just a few examples of traditions that acknowledge the value of their spirit guides, yet their helping spirits manifest in diverse ways. This makes writing an article on nonhuman spirit helpers or guides anything but straightforward or simple. Here are examples that include plants.

- One Cheyenne medicine man claimed, "If a plant radiates a blue light, it is a sign that the plant spirit wants to make contact with you. If you don't understand it, then wait until it appears to you in a dream. If you still don't understand it, then ask your grandmother. She will know" (Muller-Ebeling et al., 2003, p. 33).

- A component of Amazonian healing ways includes a ritual process (known as *dieta*), which grows one's relationship with plants in such a way so that the plant informs his or her thoughts, dreams, and character. Teacher plants vary and are for specific purposes, such as treating cancer or skin infections or general wellness maintenance and healing as well as metaphysical purposes. Whether in dreaming or waking states, acquiring such knowledge comes with expected discipline or some form of reciprocation. Breaking the rules has consequences on more than just the physical plane (Pinchbeck & Rokhlin, 2019).
- According to some legends, rainforest shamans received preparation instructions from the ayahuasca vine in dreams, as it would have otherwise been nearly impossible to figure out the medicinal brew's intricate recipe, given the 40,000-plus plants of the Amazon rainforest (Pinchbeck & Rokhlin, 2019).

Here are a handful of diverse examples that speak to these concepts regarding animals.

- Some dated documents reflect how European women used herbal concoctions to assist in their shamanic arts, allowing them to soul travel (conscious dream, OBE, etc.) with an entourage and even take animal form. The woman's soul could slip into an animal and travel about the forest (Muller-Ebeling et al., 2003). Others rode on animal familiars—those they were connected to in soul.
- According to one Brule Sioux legend, a man consults a coyote ally upon awakening from a dream.
- Appearing in the form of an eagle, a Lamista shaman communicates with an apprentice who has taken the form of a jaguar (Pinchbeck & Rokhlin, 2019).
- A god to Neolithic Europeans was a stag, the animal form of the sun.
- A spider spoke of the gift he would give to the old woman

Nokomis, of Chippewa (Ojibwe) legend, for saving his life. That gift was a magical silvery web made to snare bad dreams, while allowing good ones to move through.

• A Lakota Sioux legend tells of Iktomi (trickster and teacher) appearing in the form of a spider to an elder during a vision. Iktomi gifted the elder with a web spun inside a willow hoop. The evil in dreams passes through the hole while the good in dreams is captured in this web of life.

For many groups, plant and animal helpers are important, as both can provide the "song" needed to cure. Here is an example:

Shamans native to the Amazon can acquire their powers in various ways, one way being from plant and animal spirits. These spirits hold unique magical chants and melodies (some with very specific healing functions) taught to shamans in dream, trance and visionary states during initiation and throughout the lifetime. Through the melodies and chants a shaman may merge with an animal or simply call forth the spirit, as its very essence is in the magic melody (Luna, 1992).

The animal (and sometimes plant) helping spirits may be specific and unique depending on the particular group. Additionally, the cultural and ritual contexts should be given attention. According to the old Scandinavian religion, all people have a spirit guardian or double which could be seen in dreams. For the Scandinavian shaman, it was often the wolf. Similarly, the notion of a spirit animal double was commonplace throughout Europe, along with spirit flight and shapeshifting. Medicine women of Italy assumed the form of an owl. In Greece, the serpent gave knowledge and transformative powers (Dashu, 2016). Even though these geographical locations are fairly close, one can see that the particular animal named here is not the same. Moving across the world, however, we may see one or more of these animals (wolf, owl, serpent) as significant to that distant, distinct society. The very notion of such alliances radically challenge Western worldviews.

Initially, and for some groups even today, these animal or plant helping manifestations were seen as a type of guardian, then later, with the spread of Christianity, interpreted as an evil force used to blame or scapegoat. Some believed that women were given herbal knowledge by the devil—an exchange for lewd acts. It's no surprise that women were the top target. The Christian bias against women still felt today can be traced to disobedience or original sin—a theory created by Saint Augustine of Hippo just a few hundred years after Christ. Many had to go along with the new Christianized interpretations or suffer harsh consequences. Herbal knowledge, the wearing of animal masks and skins, and dream interpretation were so commonplace that books and declarations, such as the eighth-century Latin Declaration on the Superstitions and the Countryfolk, as well as other penance books of the time, instructed missionaries on how to punish non–Christianized European tribal groups. It is no surprise that areas of the world left unaffected have carried forward with their traditional ways relatively unscathed. During the months when I was completing my yoga nidra certification, one of the Indian instructors reminded me that India did not live through the Dark Ages, as Europe had. While there were many struggles alongside the nasty impact of imperialism, yogic scripture and spirituality continued to develop—it wasn't stunted in the manner that the traditional ways of Europe had been. The same could be said for the Americas. European colonization, as noted above, is directly responsible for the lost writings produced by Indigenous Americans.

The following terms are *not interchangeable, yet there is some overlap* when considering the purpose or function of a familiar spirit, familiar animal, spirit guardian, tutelary spirit, fylgja, or animal helping spirit. These have often served a family, clan, or community, representing a larger spiritual culture. This is in opposition to the post-enlightenment Western concept of individualism. We can see the ungrounded drain-off from this, as today, contemporary secular youngsters make explicit claims such as "XYZ is *my* spirit animal" (XYZ being either animal, object, or indulgence, such as "coffee is my spirit animal"). And next week, it's a new one. This behavior reeks of the disconnection to the dreaming world, painful histories, and unseen forces. Furthermore, we are talking about helpers who protect, instruct or guide those along a deep and profound journey.

They are not just animals with traits one needs or possesses or has an affinity or a preference for, as seen by today's common use of the term. Hence, new age "spirit animal" appropriation, centered on the individual, is ill-informed and misguided. Most often, spirit helpers choose us, usually in a time of need or transition—we do not choose them. Even so, a spiritually integrated life cannot be turned off and on when one finds it to be convenient. Spirit does not work that way. These helpers require sustenance (see the following section on feeding) and lifelong commitment. Guidance and creative ideas, dreams and visions grow out of the imaginal realm, alternate dimensions, and the otherworld. Those who rest in these sacred spaces understand that time does not follow linearly and that spiritual guidance does not succumb to our "imagined" clock. Let's look at some ways to go about sustaining and nurturing our relationship with the plant and animal spirits that help us.

TWELVE

Feeding Spirit Allies

IN THIS CHAPTER, I'll share with you some experiences along with thoughts about honoring, caring for, and building strong functional relationships with the spirit allies that appear to us in trance or vision, deep meditation, dream or shamanic journey. Animals, known pets or nondomestic creatures encountered in the great outdoors, may appear to us—when this occurs we can claim their power, or vital energy, so long as we care for them through honoring and feeding. Sometimes we need that vital animal power to heal an ailment in our own body. In order to "shapeshift the energy body and project energy forms that can operate at a distance from the physical body," significant ongoing relations with animal guardians is necessary (Moss, 2005, p. 198). This is not symbolic; instead it is a true working energetic connection—one that can bring forth healing on several levels, emotional, spiritual, psychic or otherwise, assisting in the integration of lost or disowned parts of ourselves.

Some years ago, when power animals began to appear in my dreams, I was naïve in that I had assumed these carnivorous animals would not require anything from me. I went on about my life, as a vegetarian primarily, not giving much attention to these animals in my everyday life. It was as if I believed these spirit allies would help me, offering assistance in a dream or shamanic journey, yet not need anything in return. After some experiences left me certain that I had a special connection with a North American cougar (aka mountain lion, puma, panther), I had an unforgettable dream.

Cougar slowly approaches me one evening on a quiet city street. I offer some food from a plastic container I'm carrying, likely full of pasta or salad. I peel back the edge of the container lid to offer a snack to this cougar—it seems calm and friendly enough. The cougar takes a quick smell and turns his head, then walks off in the distance. I felt snubbed.

Waking up that morning, I was confused and felt as if I missed something important. After all, I was snubbed by a wild dream cat! The following year, in an intense dream, the cougar appeared again.

I'm in a parking garage with my sister. Having said goodbye to her, I now walk to my car. We are on one of the higher-level floors. I notice that there is an angry cougar. Its companion just died right there next to us on the cement floor. Was I a threat? Was the cougar protecting its counterpart that had died? Suddenly, I was attacked. My sister uses her cell phone to call for help. She is several stalls down, by her car door. I defend myself, by getting on the ground, on my back in a defensive position. Cougar is fast and pounces. I wrestle the cougar, one arm around its neck and another in its mouth. I have unbelievable strength to survive such an attack. Three men pull up in a truck—they work there. The men surround us and I see that their intention is to kill the cougar. One of the men holds a strange looking gun that appears more like a spear gun than a rifle. I beg and plead for the cougar's life, while the cougar is in a submission hold underneath me. I plead to the men that they choose tranquilizing instead of annihilating this wild cat. They shoot something into the cougar's back and I am uncertain at that moment whether the cougar is dying or just falling asleep. I feel the cougar's muscles and posture relax and soften. I release him. The animal's body is relocated downstairs and my sister and I go to the ground floor where the parking garage office is located. After additional confusion, I feel myself waking up with watery eyes.

Now lying in my bed, I am stunned that I survived such an attack without cuts, broken bones, or the need for medical care in the dream. I am also shocked that a cougar would even allow me to show greater strength than he and remain in a submission hold. I cried in bed that morning, not from fear, but from an inner knowing that an important communication had taken place and that a relationship existed that I had not attended to or fully understood. After this dream, I no longer set Cougar on the back burner. I began working with this animal in both waking and dream states. How? Well, I started to take action on behalf of the developing relationship between Cougar and me and to honor the dream and nourish this animal ally. First, I studied this animal by reading as much as I could on its habits, diet, territory, and way of life as well as its meaning to indigenous peoples of the Americas since they share territory with Cougar. Soon after, I attended several dream workshops. In one workshop, participants were instructed to recreate the dream scene by "sculpting" the dream scene and characters with glue and an assortment of scrap objects (bits of wood, twigs, tissue paper, beads). I found what I needed to construct miniatures of the alive and dead cougar, myself and my sister, and the three men with their weapon. Next, we partnered up and used our creations to tell the story to the witness. From there, the process continued. Today, the miniature cougar sculpture lives in my bedroom shrine so I always remember. In another workshop, two-dimensional art was used to reconnect to the dream. By drawing, collaging or painting the scene, we can gain insight into the situation. So that is what I did, not only during the workshop but also afterward.

In yet another workshop, I was led in shamanic journeying through the use of a drum. Cougar quickly appeared, taking a seat next to me on my left side. Someone at the workshop stated that Cougar is a guardian associated with the north medicine wheel direction. When I researched this, I learned that the cougar is the animal assigned to my birthday in a Native American zodiac system. Another person reminded me that cougars are carnivores. I spoke with workshop leader, Robert Moss, about my conflict—I believe that a plant-based diet is the healthiest for humans and most important for the survival of the planet, so meat consumption was difficult and posed a true internal conflict for me. Moss suggested that I not make any changes to my day-to-day diet and preferences, but that at times, once a month, perhaps, I eat for the cougar. I nodded at the creative way to take care of this dream ally while my brainy, logical side had a mental tantrum over the contradiction. However, my sensitive nature understood completely and knew exactly what to do. Earlier that week, in fact, I was visiting friends in the Southwest who live close to the traditional way. When sharing my confusion surrounding my dreams and visions with this cougar, one friend exclaimed, "We hunted and ate a cougar once." Surprised, I asked more questions and the conversation continued. Some eat the organs of wild animals to "feed" the animal spirit ally, honoring its needs, I learned. This type of consumption is not necessarily for flavor or enjoyment. Often the flesh or organ is raw. Weaving all of these ideas and this guidance together in my mind, I purchased buffalo jerky and consumed a small piece. I simply wanted to try something different, beyond my usual habits and behaviors. Would my waking state actions encourage Cougar to remain close? Even though I grew up eating organ meat regularly, it had been over 25 years since I had consumed more than a small bite of red meat, and I was worried that I might fall ill or feel nauseous, yet I did not. As I chewed the foreign-flavored dried meat, I thought, *"This one's for you, Cougar."* I'm sure you can tell that this animal is important to me. It wasn't until a few years later that my medical team encouraged me to return to consuming small amounts of animal protein and enzymes as part of my healing regimen. I continue to do so today.

So that was my entry into feeding animal spirit allies. Nowadays, I make this a more ritualized practice. In addition, I offer Cougar gifts and a home of sorts. To the best of my ability, I make the necessary adjustments in my life according to the dream cougar's messages. During dreaming, I want to see Cougar alive, thriving and healthy, not slow, malnourished, yearning, or half-dead. In this physical waking reality, the apparent contradiction lives, all the while I know that our soul travels at night, when we sleep. Things are not as they seem. If we are to strengthen relationships made through our soul journeys, nourishing animal allies, we must act on behalf of the dream and sometimes take action in ways we may not have done before. Before I move on, I want to say that this does not require one to necessarily consume meat, but some type of offering should be considered. Robert Moss often declares "dreams require action." Action exists in many forms. I follow that advice best I can.

In the summer of 2019, a small, spotted wildcat appeared in a memorable dream. My immediate assumption was a cheetah, yet a young mountain lion (my typical visitor) is also spotted:

A young wildcat stands directly in front of me. I gaze into his eyes and admire the beautiful patterning of the face. It doesn't look to be very old.

I notice the sleek, thin body. We curl up together and I cast a protection circle around us as we rest and finally fall sleep in a circular formation. There is a shift in the dream. I have some awareness of the direction north and how moss grows on the north side of trees for those in the Northern Hemisphere.

I wake up recalling the vivid quality and the felt significance of this dream. I realize that there is something about wild cats that must be important, as they appear in dreams regularly (and in the recent past, about as often as serpents had). Either way, they are carnivores and so I must honor them properly.

When it comes to power animals, there is not only one right way to do things. There are many ways depending on custom and culture. Some are forbidden to kill, hunt, or eat the flesh of their power animal, as told in stories of shamans across cultures and even Celtic warrior-heroes. These taboos or restrictions may serve to reinforce connections with the spirit allies. Ignoring them, however, may lead to negative consequences, as I mentioned before. These practices might seem ridiculous to the uninitiated, as they do not understand the power and meaning behind these ways (Cowan, 1993).

Considering other ways to honor and relate with animal allies, think about movement. Dancing, sometimes around a fire, took place in several traditional societies across the globe and does even today. Dancing with the purpose of bringing on an altered state of consciousness is a shared practice among many groups from Asia to Africa. Sometimes dressing as the animal ally or enacting the specific movements of the animal is done to call, honor, increase identity with, or transform into that animal power. Think of ritual dance as an ecstatic technique prompting visions and journeys into nonordinary realms. This behavior raises powerful energy, which can be used as a healing force. Ritual power objects such as wands or riding sticks have been included in these ceremonies of movement among those in Europe and Asia. Church officials disagree, yet the keepers of folk medicine, as well as shamans, know the power of dance and how it can be of service.

Sometimes we can move rhythmically with our animal guardian

in the dream state. Two months later, in the fall of 2019, I had this dream.

> *Cougar appeared again, quickly rising to his feet to offer an embrace. I respond and we move together, swaying slowly as if to dance. I experience deep comfort and affection. As the dream fades, and my eyes begin to open, I continue to feel very relaxed, not wanting the experience to end as I lay there in my bed.*

Another way to honor animal guardians is by donating to nonprofit agencies that protect and educate. Located along Lake Tahoe's western shore, in Homewood, California, the Bear League offers help, advice, and education with regard to the protection of bears. For those that dream with domestic or feral cats, there is Sisters Animal Sanctuary in the Sacramento, California, area. While these are just two examples, sanctuaries exist nationwide and, I'm sure, would be grateful to receive a donation of any amount in honor of a deceased familiar or dream animal guardian.

Consciousness professor and psychotherapist Linda Mastrangelo agreed to sit down with me to discuss her thoughts and practices on this topic of honoring and feeding spirit allies. I first asked Mastrangelo about how she works with her clients who report dreams presenting animals and then how she supports her clients in building or continuing relationships with those dream beings.

Yes, I find it to be so invaluable and empowering for clients when they can access their own dream wisdom. This often comes in the form of animal helpers, including insects as well as mythical beings. There's nothing more powerful than engaging face to face with a dragon!

How I hold these "helpers" during sessions is with much reverence and curiosity. I tell my clients that it's so important that they don't try to overanalyze or "dissect" these helpers but rather engage with them with an open mind and spirit. I will often use the analogy of dissecting a frog. If we take apart the frog piece by piece, we are no longer left with the essence or spirit of "frog." There is nothing animated or alive to engage with.

When it comes to nightmares, this is especially important in the context of a nightmare or in waking life that might give the clients "creepy crawlies" or, even worse, phobias. I see this a lot especially with spiders and snakes. Clients will share they have a fear of them and certainly don't want them showing up in their dreams! At this point in the process I often give psychoeducation on the power of nightmares and how these beings or energies are actually parts of ourselves that we may fear or be disgusted by but now are ready to face and work with including spiritual gifts. Other times these helpers in their specific forms are allies here to share and, more importantly, activate their medicine and wisdom. This is called "shadow work" where the client can discover these gifts in themselves. We often start with how the helper showed up in the dream—was the helper huge in size or small, many or one? How did the client feel seeing this helper? Were they afraid or excited? How did they engage with it? Did they try to escape it in fear, try to kill it or were they positively engaging with it? Did it bite them, and if so, where?

So much rich material can come from engaging with these deep inquiries. Afterwards we may explore using associations, characteristics and myths of these helpers. Other times we may create art, engage in somatic work (such as Gendlin's work) or conduct dialogues with them using a Jungian technique called Active Imagination where we invite the helper to share why they are visiting the dreamer or client and what messages they have. These practices can not only shift perspectives but also allows clients to "feed" and integrate the helper's wisdom.

When I asked Mastrangelo for a memorable example, she said,

If Spider shows up, we may look at how she invites us to be the weaver of our own fate. This is often the case with Spider. I have found she arrives when the client "is giving their power away" and needs to take ownership of their life, especially when they feel overwhelmed by external forces like illness, significant losses or past abuses. Spider reminds us that we can change our fate merely by changing our perspective and the choices we make, like Spider does in the way she can navigate and weave her web. In the form of Spider, she also invites us to share our stories so we may heal and heal each other. You can see this archetype in many myths and fables like Grandmother Spider, Ariadne, Anansi, the Norns and even Charlotte from *Charlotte's Web*! I often ask if the client is interested in writing or have a strong urge to tell their story and the answer is often yes. Hopefully the client will heed the wisdom of Spider by honoring and "feeding" her through these practices.

Next, I asked Mastrangelo about her personal experiences.

I am very mindful of how these helpers show up in both the dreamtime and waking life. I am so grateful that I live in the part of the world that carries so much magic! Here in the redwood forest I have had encounters with helpers in their many forms including elemental or nature beings. Over the years their presences have opened up my mind and shifted my consciousness to the many invisible realms around us. In the hypnagogic state or threshold state between sleep and awake I have heard trees sing and experienced visits from the "little people" of the forest. I'm also very sensitive to how the land can affect our dreams especially if it's a sacred space or there is trauma tied to it. My dreams will often reflect this and give me information about what happened in this space and how I can be a part of the healing process. Like the tree-singing example, I was also able to hear singing of the miners that lived on the land many years ago. In both these experiences, I was not only sensing these spirits' presences but was being welcomed into the space.

Mastrangelo continued on to include some ways she works with these experiences.

Because I have been writing down my dreams and encounters for decades now, it has become my spiritual practice. I see it as natural as well as necessary in that I know when I don't do my practices, I "feel off," irritable and ungrounded. I "feed" them through my art as well and have created talismans from dreams that reflect specific medicine. I also use techniques like Dream Incubation where I send out an intention before bedtime to ask for guidance and knowledge. Another is Dream Mapping or exploring a series of dreams and their connections, as it can reveal the helpers that are more prevalent than others. For example, I have formed a deep relationship to big cats and snakes as they appear very frequently in my dreams. Their visits have taught me to honor my ancestral gifts as both a healer as well as a dream traveler or oneironaut. I have had continued dialogues specifically with both Snake and Panther who have shared with me that I have connections with them going back thousands of years! Their many messages include, "it is time to come out of the shadows and share your gifts with others." In one incubated snake dream, I asked to learn more about my ancient ancestors. I was visited in the dream by five snakes, one on top of the other. After drawing the image, I discovered that this was an emblem and was able to locate it on one of the menhirs in an ancient burial site of Carnac in France. I was later able to confirm that I indeed had ancestry in this part of France.

Mastrangelo shared additional experiences that have impacted her:

Other frequent helpers are more psychopompic in nature like vultures, owls, ravens and bats—psychopomps are beings that can travel to other

121

worlds or realms, as well as assist those who have passed over. These encounters showed up in dreams and waking life right before my decision to do therapeutic work at a hospice and they continue to this day. I realized I have a strong connection to the Underworld with the work that I do and often joke that in addition to being a grief therapist I have a "second job at night" practicing dream healing with those that have died and need support passing over. These spirit helpers (including actual "invisible" healers) have assisted me in my healing work (both personally and professionally) and continue to encourage and challenge me. It's powerful when I receive confirmation in dreams and waking life in forms of gifts. I have an altar showcasing some of these gifts like feathers from raven, owl and vulture and feed this spirit by conducting personal rituals where I honor and give them gratitude back. This is why I believe these connections to be both sacred as well as symbiotic.

Plant spirit allies may require diverse means, unlike the consumption of meat, as wild carnivores sometimes do. Instead, I talk to the plants in my medicine garden and project love over them. I also give them little gifts—small tokens of appreciation—such as shiny crystals or rocks that I have painted with attractive geometric designs. Those with other talents might sing to or play soft instruments for plants or recite poems inspired by a particular plant helper. Other times, I plant additional plants nearby so they have company. Most importantly, I slow down, sense, and listen, not just in the daytime but in dreamtime as well. If we make agreements with plant and animal allies, it's important to understand their rules and limits. What are their conditions?

Southern California naturopathic doctor Sunshine Weeks agreed to share her knowledge of nature with me. I asked, "Since you work closely with plants, herbs, and flowers, how have they shown up for you, or communicated with you, in vision or dream, meditation, intuitive or prayer states?" Dr. Weeks replied,

When I am making a formula for a patient and standing there looking at the herbs sometimes one will call to me so loudly that I can't deny that it wants to be in the formula for that person. I can't explain how I hear it, it is more of a physical sensation. I don't get it for every patient but often I will just stand there and wait for them to tell me who wants to do the work for the patient. It is fun watching my students learn to listen to the plants. When we formulate there are some plants that work well in combination for a patient and they will almost volunteer. You can always tell an herbal formula is going to work when it looks pretty in the bag or container. Things that look appealing to the eye tend to be more balanced. So the plants talk to me all the time.

"Do you feel that there is a relationship between you and the plants you most often use due to your close work with them in the healing profession?" I asked. "I have also found that plant medicines work differently once there is a relationship with them," she replied. "Once a student develops a relationship with a plant that plant will do amazing things both for them and their patients. They do things that before that relationship they wouldn't have done. Some plants like loud people who talk to them and especially like to be sung to, while others like it if you just sit there and wait for their quiet voice. The Ribbonwood out here is very quiet to me, but lavender loves chatting."

I also asked, "How have you 'fed' them? I mean, how do you give back in order to keep the communication, or helping relationship, flowing?"

I love the topic of giving back to and honoring plants. Reciprocity is very welcome in the plant world. Sometimes when harvesting a plant, they are just grateful for a thoughtful trimming when taking plant material. They seem to feel like they just got a new haircut. Water, of course, is probably our most common gift in return, but the Celtic folks used to give a little gift of milk. Some Native Americans will give an offering of tobacco which is crumbled and scattered in the wind. Tobacco connects the human world with the plant world so we can learn more clearly from them and hear what they need. Prayers are another gift for plants, prayers that they will be strong and prosperous are received in the same way as we receive those kinds of prayers.

There are plants who are amazingly generous like the elderberry, it gives and gives and gives, flowers, fruit, shade. It is called the elder because other plants like to grow under it and it protects them. Other plants have less to give so you have to be more careful but their medicine can be very strong. I have students that are undeniably drawn to certain plants. I find that they call to me more subtly than some of my students who feel a connection so intensely. Plants have clear personalities both as a species and as individuals. I have felt the best hug from a Blue Spruce. Sometimes plants just mind their own business, but some are very outgoing.

With regard to dreaming, she added, "I don't remember my dreams very often but the artemisias [mugwort, wormwood, sagebrush and more] are great with helping people dream."

Plants stand outside themselves, living between the worlds of mineral and animal. Interacting with plants can best take place during soul flight, where one mystically transcends in order to merge with the ecstatic plant world. The soul of a sentient plant may be sensed the most in its flower (Muller-Ebeling et al., 2003). The earth is very much alive. We can train ourselves to become increasingly sensitive and open to perceiving the earth's messages by slowing down, minimizing our consumption, spending time in nature, and by building relationships just as we would with other elements or forces of nature. Most importantly, we would not destroy that from which we desire relations, so making a personal commitment to care for this living planet is essential and non-negotiable.

THIRTEEN

Sleep Hygiene

S LEEP IS SO FUNDAMENTAL to a well-lived life. Sleep hygiene: it's a term we've heard before—we find it surfacing more and more these days in blogs and other online articles. So what is it all about? Sleep hygiene encompasses healthy practices—making behavioral and environmental adjustments—for solid, restful, good-quality sleep. Millions of Americans report sleep disturbances. In fact, many of my clients come in for their first appointment telling me that getting five to six hours of sleep a night is typical for them. This is a call for change. Chronic sleep deprivation is associated with a long list of physiological and psychological problems as well as illness and disease onset. In fact, research suggests that REM/dream loss contributes to an "erosion of consciousness" and substances used by many to facilitate sleep, such as alcohol and cannabis, "can negatively impact REM/dreaming" (Naiman, 2017, p. 77). There are so many good reasons to prioritize sleep. Anyone who wants to practice dream medicine understands this.

A consistent sleep hygiene routine helps the mind and body recognize that bedtime is approaching and that it is time to wind down. I'll list some common sleep hygiene practices below—what to do and what to avoid.

Many people do one or more of these about an hour or two before bedtime:

- Take a warm shower or bath.
  - ◊ A bath ritual can be as simple as adding a teaspoon or two of sea salt to the bath water. You can also add about 5–10 drops of pure, organic essential oil (I like combining lavender with clary sage or lavender with sandalwood).

Why not toss in a handful of herbs or flowers from your garden too?

- Read a pleasant book.
  - ◊ Even if you normally enjoy thrillers, now is not the time. Preparing for restful sleep doesn't pair well with such stimulation.
- Make it tea time!
  - ◊ Chamomile tea is the go-to bedtime ritual for many tea lovers. However, there are other herbs and flowers that can bring about a relaxing effect. I drink tea throughout the day, but I especially enjoy it in the evening, as it helps me wind down. Naturopathic physician Dr. Sunshine Weeks is a lover of plants with a great amount of herbal knowledge. She shared with me one of her preferred combinations. Dr. Weeks blends passion flower, lemon balm, and ashwagandha together in order to create a tea for consumption as part of a bedtime ritual. Passion flower is absolutely gorgeous to look at—I find it quite stunning—and can be a helper when it comes to sleep hygiene. Passion flower supports a calming and relaxing effect, thus promoting healthy sleep. Related to the mint family, lemon balm promotes a sense of calm, preparing the body for rest. Ashwagandha is an adaptogen, promoting homeostasis and normal sleep patterns. If you are pregnant do not use ashwagandha. Instead combine the first two ingredients: lemon balm and passion flower only! Again, this information is for general reference and should not be a substitution for medical advice. Consult your physician before consumption.
- Do some light stretches.
  - ◊ No need for a formal asana yoga routine. Any kind of gentle stretching will do. Some people even enjoy getting on the floor and using rollers. The point is to get out of the head and into the body any way that suits you and supports winding down.
- Write in a journal.

◊ Journaling has become very popular. One journaling prompt could be to make a five-point gratitude list. Another could be to free write about a good memory from that day—just let it flow.

- Listen to relaxing music.
  - ◊ It doesn't have to be classical. If you enjoy it and it helps release tension from the day, then you've got the right idea. If you have a significant other, why not slow dance while you're at it?
- Dim the lights, or at least turn some off.
  - ◊ Overhead lighting can be stimulating. It can also remind us of the office. By using a floor or table lamp for lighting, the mood will shift. Give it a try.
- Engage in well-known relaxation practices such as mindfulness or autogenics.
  - ◊ Sitting with awareness of our breath can be very relaxing. Try a few dozen rounds of mindful breathing. Track each inhalation or exhalation. Can you make it to 25? How about 35?
  - ◊ Autogenic training is used in order to gain control of autonomic arousal. Simply put, autogenics calms the nervous system. I like focusing on my limbs, one at a time, using "warm and heavy" as my suggestions.
- Make a list.
  - ◊ If a lot is weighing on your mind and there are tasks you want to remember, make a note or a list for yourself. That way, the thought is captured on paper and can be released mentally. This has been so helpful in my life.

Here is what to avoid in the evening or at least one hour or more before bed:

- Electronic use/screen time
- Social media
- Stimulating films or television shows
- Altering substances such as alcohol, caffeine and nicotine

- Stimulating conversations or arguments
- Consuming a lot of liquid
- Bright lighting
- Loud music
- Vigorous exercise
- Work that requires focus and concentration as it can be stimulating and invoke a stress response

Above all:

- Dedicate the bedroom for sleeping, dreaming, and sex, instead of a place associated with work or mentally stimulating activity.
- Turn the bedroom into a relaxation oasis.
- Avoid early evening naps.
- Go to bed around the same time every night, preferably before midnight. A consistent sleep schedule sets the body's internal clock.

Everything listed above can be supportive for quality sleep and deeply restorative rest. Now if a particular dream technique will be practiced, such as one for lucid dreaming, dream re-entry, or dream incubation, additional sleep hygiene will likely be helpful. This includes keeping the bedroom clean and free of clutter. In addition, dedicate the space to living the dream arts. I dive in deep. For example, in my bedroom, I have small statues of goddesses and archangels most important to me, a candle or two, my most treasured crystals, organic essential oil sprays including Florida Water, my tarot cards, a flat slab of selenite, herbs for smelling or burning (primarily mugwort), cute placards with messages about dreaming, a glass of water—all this in addition to a small dream altar. These are my personal preferences and by no means necessary or meaningful for anyone else. Naturally, create your own space that is tailored to your belief system and preferences.

Fourteen

Dream Incubation

SOMETIMES WE CAN JUST FALL ASLEEP with a problem on our mind, or one we believe we have forgotten about, only to wake up the next morning with a solution. Has this happened to you? It's more common than you think! Other times, we may set an intention for dream guidance, meaning that we go to sleep intentionally thinking of a problem and asking for a solution to appear in the dream. Not only are these scenarios common, they also have a place throughout history across cultures. For example, *Istikhara* is Islamic dream incubation, still currently practiced throughout North Africa. It is practiced in order to generate "true" dreams and divine guidance or fortune or grace. Istikhara is used for making decisions related to marriage, mating, business, politics, and economic affairs (Edgar, 2006; Gonzalez-Vazquez, 2014).

Here is a striking contemporary dream incubation example from Barrett's 1993 research:

> *Problem*: I have applied to two clinical psychology programs and two in industrial psychology because I just can't decide which field I want to go into.
> *Dream*: A map of the United States, and I'm in a plane flying over this map. The pilot says we're having engine trouble and need to land. We look for a safe place on the map indicated by a light. I ask about Massachusetts, which we're right over, but he says that all of Massachusetts is very dangerous. The lights seemed to be further west.
> *Solution*: I woke up and realized that my two clinical schools are both in Massachusetts where I've spent my whole life and where my parents live. Both industrial programs are far away, in Texas and California. This is because originally I was looking to stay close to home and there were no good industrial programs nearby. I realized that there is a lot wrong with staying at home and, funny as it sounds, getting away is probably

more important than which kind of program I go into [Barrett, 2017, p. 66].

If this student were experiencing stress and the accompanying ailments, then this would be an example of what I think of as incubated dream medicine. However, we have a more benign situation here. This student successfully incubated a dream which provided guidance and appears to have even given the okay signal for the outcome this student truly desired. This resolution may be due to the dichotomous situation—two clear, well-defined choice points.

Incubating Health

Dream incubation can be utilized for greater health concerns as well. Possible questions or statements to pose include:

- "Show me a solution to this problem (or situation or issue)."
- "Show me a mirror that can allow me to see into my body, revealing health or illness."
- "What area of my life needs my attention right now?"

I spoke with Dr. Clare Johnson and Dr. Bhaskar Banerji in early 2020 regarding the use of dreams in the healing process. Johnson's 2018 book, *Mindful Dreaming,* is a must read! She knows the power dreams can harness and the healing energy they can provide. Johnson dedicates an entire chapter to illness and pain, offering ways to "dream yourself well." Banerji tested this out. His 2017 doctoral research focused on how dreams can evoke one's inner healing resources. About 100 people with a chronic illness participated in his study involving dream incubation. Before bed, participants listened to a dream incubation recording, and the following morning they were prompted to fill out a form in order to log their recollections. From this process, three healing categories emerged, what Banerji labeled "Insight," "Experiential," or "Prescription." The category "Insight" described dreams that provide some sort of insight into the healing process. The "Experiential" category included dreams where an actual healing experience was reported to occur. "Prescription" was the category for dreams in which instruction, direction or other explicit information was given. In fact, a series of the dreams reported by several participants included all three categories in that same order: Insight, Experiential, followed by Prescription healing dreams. Both Johnson and Banerji believe that people have the ability to use dream incubation in order to assess current health conditions. Since all people dream, we have nightly opportunities to enhance healing conditions within (Johnson, 2018).

During late 2018, 2019, and 2020, my dream journals were filled with both symbolism and metaphor as well as direct messages likely regarding the state of my health. The vast majority of my notes and sketches were taken from nocturnal dream experiences, many of them incubated, yet a few emerged out of dream-like visionary states from experiences with shamanic journeying and guided imagery. When it came to health metaphors and symbolism, I noted dozens of messages and images, mostly related to malfunctioning phones, an overheating vehicle, a chart with info related to health, my home being invaded, cobwebs needing to be cleared away, and my body being submerged in thick, wet mud as well as images of clogged or overflowing toilets or dirty pools, ponds or lakes. Here is one recollection paraphrased from my dream journal in March of 2019:

> *I'm in my vehicle and I'm the driver. I safely arrive at my destination but it's overheated. I see the little symbol lit up indicating that the vehicle was operating too high. I worry about how I will get back/make the return trip. It's best to drive slower and not use the air-conditioning system. It is necessary to look out for how much I drive and the manner in which I drive. This can prevent overheating.*

I believe Banerji would place these types of dreams into the Insight category, as they provided great insight. In these dreams I recognized the need for repair or for cleaning as well as slowing down and being mindful. Another example came from a dream, also in March of 2019, seven months before my diagnosis. Here is how that dream began:

> *I'm in a house—it must be winter because of the heavy amount of snow. My parents are around. We eat dinner together as the sun sets. I ask them about the weird phenomenon occurring in the neighborhood. They don't give me straight answers. I walk away irritated. After I press on and demand answers they tell me that I must keep the "right foot on the ground" to remain safe. I find this to be a strange response. I'm not even sure what the danger actually is!*

But what was I to do day to day, in the physical waking state? Of course, internal cleansing and repairing came to mind. Should I do a fast? Take more salt-water baths? Increase my hours of sleep? Return to psychotherapy? Enroll in a meditation class? Schedule a physical or request blood work? After a series of similarly themed dreams—those telling me that something was out of order and to slow it down—one dream from February of 2020 in particular stood out. The following dream led me to begin a detoxification process— one that was even more intense than what I had done in the past. Even though there were no vehicles in the dream, at the very start of the dream I realize

> *I need a catalytic converter. My Uncle X appears and places the order. When they arrive, I see that there are many of them. There are more than I believe I need, but he tells me, "that's how they come, in a package."*

As the dream fades and I begin to awaken, we are negotiating over how many I should pay for and I feel annoyed.

Other dreams revealed that I was preparing to ride a roller coaster and traveling—taking long trips or journeys. Could these earlier dreams have been providing clues for what to expect or prepare for? No surprise, given the nature of chronic illnesses. They don't "clean up" as quickly as a broken arm.

In later dreams, after beginning to make some life adjustments (yet with so many more to come), I get some help—help that I understand and can recall. I'm shown special plants and given a healing elixir, an elaborate colorful necklace holding great significance, and a spiraling staff to act as some sort of weapon. And in other dreams, instruction was offered by somewhat more direct messages (aka Prescription healing dreams according to Banerji): one told me, plain and simple, to eat more cauliflower; another dream directed me to eat collard greens—a green leafy vegetable I had never consumed before; and another showed me how to use a slow/cold-press juicer and the best combination of vegetables to use. These dream instructions were easy to follow—I immediately purchased this type of juicer and began consuming greater quantities of vegetables. In reference to his research, Banerji told me, "almost half the prescription dreams took the form of dietary recommendations highlighting the important role food choices play in ensuring our health and wellness" (personal communication, January 25, 2020). This point has never been more clear.

In addition, one dream told me to spend more time in nature and eat organically, and yet another dream revealed a specific type of drum needed for healing (a large shamanic style drum). Here is an excerpt from that particular dream:

> *A suggestion arises about something I need. I am walking outside looking for a sign. I'm emotional and have an awareness of the illness. I bump into someone I know. I am supposed to find a shamanic drummer, and there she is holding one, but it is three times the size—I'm used to smaller ones. The frame is as tall as almost the length of her body. I have an inner knowing that this is what I am supposed to be doing or finding. I cry. It's emotional. I feel this as I awaken.*

In several other dreams I actively practiced setting limits, assertiveness, and held strong boundaries with irresponsible, overbearing, or demanding dream characters. Changes all around, especially in the ways in which I care for my body and mind.

Dreams also showed me what to avoid. My good friends know how much I adore a quality bakery and delight in all sorts of breads and pastries (or at least I used to). In one particular dream, I passed by a bakery and noticed beautifully shaped sugar cookies. I looked closer at them to appreciate the details and what do you know—they were in the shape of human skulls. I had an awareness in that dream that I was not to eat any sugar at all, as it could lead to my early death. An even earlier dream featured gourmet sandwiches, which I rejected. I preferred not to eat anything in the dream. In the waking state, it would have been difficult for me to resist a sandwich like that! Now, I avoid bread, white foods, and almost everything that converts to sugar in the body when consumed.

Another message came through in that familiar liminal space, the hypnopompic state, just as I was waking up. One morning, a particular auditory message came through in a feminine-sounding voice reminding me of the "body's innate wisdom to heal itself." This prompted me to do more yoga nidra (aka yogic sleep) and make it a practice I engage in on most days.

Other experiences included wild animals, either injured or, quite the opposite, offering support. Yet, through a serious, and perhaps fatal, illness I felt protected to some degree. Even so, you can bet I was uneasy. The cougar/mountain lion appeared most often, offering affection, hugs, and a dance, or just simply to sit by my side or sleep alongside my body. I considered ways I could sustain and thank this dream ally. In one lucid dream, I asked about the root of the condition I was diagnosed with and an alien's face—not quite a wild animal—manifested in front of me while in that same lucid dream the way to heal was shown to be through meditative states. Once again, the need for stress reduction, empowerment, and insight became clear. I knew it was my time for action. My dreams were to become my guiding compass, my main medicine. Just as I wondered if I was even remotely on the right track—wishing for a fast track toward healing—I had a dream showing me that I could flush a toilet. It was no longer clogged or overflowing, as previous dreams had reflected. In this dream I even flushed that toilet twice! This dream came in April 2020, just a little over a year after the dream of my overheating vehicle, and a couple months after the catalytic converter dream.

In early November 2020, when considering whether to get another MRI sooner rather than later, all the while weighing the pros and cons of risking COVID exposure from visiting a major medical center, I fell asleep with this question on my mind. The next morning I recalled a dream showing me a physician I had never met. I was surprised because I rarely dream of medical professionals. In the dream, the physician was a white, middle-aged female, about my height, with short, brown hair cut into the style of a bob. I sense she is an N.D. (a naturopathic doctor). She holds an unfamiliar device in her hand used to measure tumor size. I ask her if I should rush to get an MRI done. She says, "Nah, no rush." I woke up in bed that morning with a diminished sense of urgency and feeling that my current treatment plan was good enough for the time. While I still planned to get an MRI, I was no longer anxious about the exact timing.

Even with all of this internal dream support, I did not hesitate to ask others who dream strong for some help. I figured if others I trusted could enter my dreams and provide or transmit healing energy to me in that space, why not ask and accept? When much of one's support system lives across the state or the country (or even in a different country than your own), it can be quite convenient to work together in the dream state, offering support. Shared dreaming and mutual dreaming happen all the time. Some people make a distinction between these two terms. For instance, when two people wake up and share their dreams with each other, they may notice that certain dream elements appear in both dreams—that's usually referred to as shared dreaming. "Shared dreams occur when the dreamers meet one another in the exact same place and time within a dream that occurred on the same night" (McNamara et al., 2017, p. 88). However, when two (or more) people experience a similar dream and interact with one another in that dream, or believe that it was the same dream, well, that's mutual dreaming, and it's fascinating! When it comes to wellness, it takes a community. When times are tough, don't hesitate to ask for support from those you admire, care for or respect, even if the support given comes by way of a dream. To this day, I am very grateful to those who agreed to offer healing dream assistance when I was in need.

I recall Robert Moss once saying that "dreams are body talk as well as soul talk" and that dreams basically hold up a magic mirror. It is through the art and practice of dreaming that we can see into our own depths and discover what is needed for sustenance as well as personal and transpersonal growth. When we need a boost, others are often willing to give a hand and lift us.

Incubation Techniques

There are several ways to incubate dreams. According to Barrett in her *New York Times* interview, there is a high level of success for those practicing dream incubation (Weaver, 2020). Here is just one popular way to go about it. Write your question or clearly stated request on a piece of paper or an index card, state it aloud, place the paper under your pillow, and mentally repeat what you have written as your body relaxes. Stay alert enough to catch solutions whether sounds or images may arise before drifting off to sleep. This pre-sleep zone is rich in what it can offer. On that note, be aware when you are awakening as well, as it is another valuable time period for gaining insights and catching solutions. Remain physically still as your awareness rises in order to enhance dream recall. Anything that you remember should be recorded along with a quick rough sketch so that when you stand up and other distractions arise, they do not steal the dream's precious offerings. This, at its essence, is dream incubation.

Another way to practice the art of dream incubation is to choose the one or two days a week that dream incubation will be practiced. On those days, avoid alcohol or other drugs as well as screen time and heavy foods in the evening. Perhaps consider sleeping in a different space those nights, especially if your bedmate snores or shifts around a lot. With that said, there is no need to treat this practice as if a final exam were approaching. These are just ideas. Like all consciousness-heightening activity, use self-compassion and proceed with care. You can enhance your dream incubation practice further by taking a relaxing bath before bedtime. Perhaps even add some light stretching and gentle movement, journaling, meditation, or prayer. Use candles and safe essential oils if that's right for you. These days, my preference for setting the tone is a combination of what I consider to be most relaxing: beeswax candles, pure organic lavender essential oil infused salt water baths, and breathwork (particularly an inhalation-exhalation cycle at a 4:8 ratio). Preparing for sleep and shedding the day's residue is personal—there is no one correct way. Just go with what feels right as long as it is safe and healthy. Intend to be helped by your dreams. In exchange, behave as if you are about to participate in an ancient healing ritual ... because, well, you are.

Fifteen

Dream Reentry

Artist and scientist Fariba Bogzaran is one of the authors of *Extraordinary Dreams and How to Work with Them*. In the chapter "Healing Dreams," she shares how she has used dreams not only as diagnostic tools but also as a means for healing. She tells the story of her experience in flu season when she felt she was on the verge of illness. During a nap, she had a dream:

> *I am walking in a street and suddenly I am attacked by ferocious groups of bugs. I am trying to defend myself but they are too aggressive. I become more and more anxious* [Krippner et al., 2002, p. 74].

She awoke from the nap with a sore throat and headache. What might such a dream be telling a person about illness susceptibility? Bogzaran went into action. She used a technique known as dream reentry.

Dream reentry is a technique developed by Robert Moss. He describes the technique alongside several experiences in his 1996 book *Conscious Dreaming: A Spiritual Path for Everyday Life* and his 2005 book *Dreamways of the Iroquois: Honoring the Secret Wisdom of the Soul*. Dream reentry opens the dreamer up to new images that may appear, along with interactions with dream objects and characters. Yes, that's right, I said characters. Everything is alive in dreams, so you may question and dialogue with everything. The same is true for visions. In my dream reentry experiences (some led by Robert Moss, creator of active dreaming) I have either questioned or dialogued with snakes, books, tables, deceased people, airplane exhaust, spiders ... you get the idea. Know that this is a conscious process quite different from controlling or interfering with the dream in any way.

Using this technique, Bogzaran re-entered the dream, continuing to walk up that street. This time, though, she extended her arms as the bugs approached her so that she could imagine repelling them by the liquid stream shooting out from her fingers. This direct, defensive action resulted in her body feeling lighter—most of the bugs were successfully repelled. When she ended the dream reentry, her headache was gone. Within just a few hours, the soreness in her throat had gone away and she was feeling a whole lot better. The flu didn't get her that season!

Bogzaran is very experienced, so if you begin practicing dream reentry only to find that images are blurry and attention fades, do not fret. These things take practice. Still, even with a recalled dream fragment, such as a bright red flower or a singing bird, you can use that fragment as your point of reentry. This isn't much different from other memory fragments, such as ones you have from years past.

Curious to give dream reentry a shot? One of the best times to try this technique is immediately after waking up, so if you can sleep in one morning a week or schedule time for an extended late morning nap, that would be ideal. If that is impossible, try for later that day, perhaps on a lunch break. Interruptions happen, but they won't help you when reentering a dream, so silence phones and alarms if possible.

Moss (1996), who has been helping people reenter their dreams for decades, says that two things are necessary for successful dream reentry: "your ability to focus clearly on a remembered scene from your dream, and your ability to relax and allow your consciousness to flow back inside the scene" (p. 65). When on my own, I use self-hypnosis to reenter a dream or vision. When I've been with Robert Moss or Fariba Bogzaran, shamanic drumming has been used, as they both support their workshop participants with this highly effective and very traditional method. Either way, prepare for dream reentry by choosing a dream or vision that has some charge, some real energy behind it, explains Moss (2005). Maybe something exciting! Reflect, then ask yourself, "What do I want to know?" Is there anything I need to do?" Refer to the two books listed above for specific instructions by Robert Moss. Here, I will share the way I go about this practice, which has been adapted from many years of learning from different teachers and colleagues of diverse backgrounds (hypnosis, spiritual/transpersonal psychology, yoga nidra, gnostic mysticism, traditional women's ways, and shamanism). Once you have asked yourself the questions listed above, proceed with the following:

- Get situated.
    - ◊ Place a notepad and pens or pencils nearby.
    - ◊ Clear the space. There are many ways to do this. I prefer lighting a pure beeswax candle and spraying a few squirts of an essential oil concoction prepared for ridding spaces of negative energy. I also like visualizing a circle of protection around the room I am using, after I am sitting or laying comfortably in the center. Other options include smoking the room (always have a couple windows cracked), placing statues of archangels or other saints around the room, or casting a circle of salt. Placing little cups of salt in each corner of the room is fine too. Hold a strong, clear intention for what you are about to do—this really matters!
    - ◊ Find a comfortable place to lay or sit if you haven't already. Recliner chairs are excellent for this, or even a padded yoga mat with soft pillows. Cover yourself with a blanket or throw since, for some, the body cools down during these practices.
    - ◊ Call in a helper or ally. Examples include a guardian angel or saint, an animal spirit or the holy spirit, Jesus, Quan Yin, or another strong force such as love.
- Tune inward.
    - ◊ Now that your body is comfortable, focus on your breath. Notice each inhalation and exhalation. Stay with the breath. Mentally tell yourself, "With each breath, I relax more and more."
    - ◊ Scan your body to look for any tightness or tension. Breathe into those spaces to support deeper relaxation.

Progressive muscle relaxation can be used at this time if
you find it helpful.

◊ Vocalize a mantra such as AUM, or use a vowel mantra—
my favorite is the letter O or A. I tone with these letters,
O or A, as I focus on my chest center and middle torso
regions. See if you can get a vibration going for a couple
minutes, then slow it down, softening the sound.

◊ Count down from 20 to 1. Tell yourself again that with
each number you relax more and more and become more
and more aware.

• Focus on the vision or dream.

◊ Go narrow now and really focus on the chosen image or
scene. Really see it in your mind's eye.

◊ Use all senses. Notice any sounds or smells? Can you feel
anything on your skin?

◊ Continue to breathe deeply to stay relaxed.

• Move forward with your intention.

◊ Ask a direct question, silently, mentally. Be clear.
Maintain awareness so you take in the response or
answer.

◊ Keep breathing.

◊ Complete any necessary action should the dream require
one.

◊ When ready, come back into the body by wiggling your
fingers and toes and opening your eyes. This is a good
time to roll over on your side in order to log or sketch
your experience.

For some people, this process is enough and allows for gaining new insights and reconnecting with the dream. For others, a little more is needed. Robert Moss, among many others, suggests
heartbeat shamanic drumming for fueling the dream reentry journey. Look online for workshops if you'd like to experience this technique. In my experience, valuable health-related information can be
obtained from vision or dream by participating in these methods. I
enjoy them all.

When it comes to using dream incubation and dream re-entry, there is a more playful side, one that may be new for many people. Dr. Angel Morgan, the past president of the IASD, is a psychologist, author and lifelong dreamer. I have had the privilege to experience one of her workshops and discuss dreams with her on several occasions, most recently through the Shift Network's 2020 Dreamwork Summit. Here are some insights into our conversations. Dreams help us get in touch with our true selves. Dream arts and creativity exist as a dual-directional flow, one inspiring and impacting the other. By acting out our dreams in "improvisational dream theater," we can assimilate and integrate those unacknowledged or unknown parts of the self, leaving the dreamer empowered in the end. It's like re-entering the dream from full waking consciousness with a small group of supportive people.

Dr. Morgan also recognizes how lucid dreaming can support musicians and actors in that they can rehearse their part for an upcoming performance in the lucid dream state in order to become more competent and confident in their role. She reminds us that being a skilled lucid dreamer is not necessary for using the dream state to support our growth through theater arts. We can simply ask for guidance on the situation through dream incubation. Furthermore, engaging in "improv dream theater" can bring insight for both lucid and non-lucid dreams—the dreamer is always the "director" and as the director he or she can choose to witness the dream theater unfold (choosing someone else to play the dreamer) or the dreamer can choose to play his or her own part from the dream. Either way, the dream belongs to the dreamer, so the director role is important to honor in this process.

Sixteen

Facing Challenges

A s ONE WALKS THE PATH of dream medicine, there will be road-blocks. We may stumble, get stuck, or need assistance from those with more experience. That's a natural part of this work and it does not reflect poorly on anyone.

When Nightmares Creep In

Nightmares, or scary dreams, are common, affecting both children and adults. Riddled with emotions, such as fear, rage, terror or grief, the dreamer is jolted awake remembering the plot, characters, and scene of the nightmare. In his book *Nightmares: The Science and Solution of Those Frightening Visions During Sleep*, neurocognitive scientist Patrick McNamara comments on nightmares and self-identity. "One constant feature of nightmares is that the self comes under attack by very powerful forces and the attack is terrifying" (2008, p. 85). Bad dreams can occur in various stages of sleep (Yu, 2020), yet it is during rapid eye movement (REM) when these frightening dreams most frequently occur (Krippner, 2016). During the COVID-19 pandemic, some people were sleeping more than they normally would. This may have led to the reports of strange dreams that filled Internet forums through the beginning of 2020. Increased sleep brings increased activity in the sleeping brain, so more vivid dreams may be recalled in these longer dream periods (Weaver, 2020). Furthermore, a pandemic is concerning, so threatening dreams where dangers lurk around every corner are not terribly surprising. Tidal waves are common during these times. Are you drowning or learning to surf? If you're a healthcare provider, says Barrett, the nightmares are likely to be more extreme (Schnalzer, 2020).

Although quite rare, lucid nightmares are known to occur. In a 2018 study, Stumbrys found that the most common features of lucid nightmares were lack of dream control and intense fear. Even though nightmares, in general, are fairly common, these frightening and uncomfortably bizarre experiences—believe it or not—can actually become the gateways for healing. We just have to know what to look for.

Some of my own disturbing, yet impactful, dreams contain natural forces, such as fire, water, or strong wind. When I was going through a tough time in my career and needed to make a big decision, a powerful tornado appeared in my dream. In the dream the tornado was really close by, just in front of me about an acre away. In the dream, I confronted it. Later, as I began to find myself waking up in my bed, the intensity was palpable. I was confused and still a bit scared. Had I really returned from the land of the tornado? After waking up more fully, I applied dreamwork techniques to the scary dream material in order to understand the experience more fully. In the end, I made a firm decision to take action, which changed the direction regarding my responsibilities and role in the nonprofit world. To heal or correct the situation I was in, I needed to face something as big and scary as a tornado. It was equivalent to the probable impact regarding the unfolding legal "situation." Not only did I confront the powerful force in the dream, I also replayed that confrontation at work in the physical waking state, with Tornado as my teacher.

When I sat down to consider which of the experienced psychotherapists I knew really understood the hidden treasure that nightmares can hold, Linda Yael Schiller came to mind immediately. We met at an IASD conference, after all. Schiller told me, "Most of us recoil in fear when we have or think about our nightmares. Who wouldn't—by definition they are scary! But our dreams and even our nightmares contain the seeds of our healing as well."

In Schiller's 2019 book, *Modern Dreamwork: New Tools for*

Decoding Your Soul's Wisdom, she introduces her readers to the concept that there is a gift in every dream, even in our nightmares. We just need to understand how to look for it. But first, Schiller says, "we need to be in a safe space in order to confront or resolve our fears in waking and dreaming life. The GAIA method of the Guided Active Imagination Approach described in my book teaches dreamers how to set up a safe container within which to do the hard yet necessary work that will allow them to gain relief from nightmares."

Remember, Schiller says, "fear is a part of the human condition, yet we are also all wired for healing and growth. If we pay attention to our nightmares and our dreams and work with them, they can provide resources and guidance."

In one of our email exchanges, Schiller wrote, "I had a dream (over a year ago) that I knew was important but didn't realize its potential until sharing it with my dream circle. The process of talking about it out loud, with some well-placed questions from my friends, helped me to recognize what had been in my blind spot before and find the healing embedded in it." Below is a portion of Schiller's dream:

> *I am driving my car on my way to meet my husband somewhere, when all of a sudden there is no light—it has become pitch dark. My car lights are gone, and there are no streetlights or even stars—nothing but blackness. This time I am surprisingly not as frightened as I could be, just a little anxious. This is different than my usual response of full out panic in such a situation. I grip the steering wheel and just keep driving up and down ramps and over passes and underpasses. Suddenly there is light again, it is daylight, and I am in a warm southern place.*

The dream continues on for a bit, Schiller says,

but this is the journey part of the dream. I come up with an initial title for it: *Driving Blind.* As I talked my way through it with my dream group, in addition to noticing my somatic responses, I realize that it is kind of like life itself—sometimes we are *driving blind*, we don't really know where we are going, but we just know that we have to keep on going through whatever this difficult time is. If we stop, if we get paralyzed by fear, we get stuck in the dark. In my dream I come out into the light at the end—if that's not a metaphor, I don't know what is. As I kept talking, I realized that the reason that I wasn't as afraid as I might have been about driving in the dark had to do with faith—I must have trusted even while driving with no lights that it would turn out ok. This is something I have been working on for years—trust and faith. I then was able to re-name the dream *Blind Faith* and bring that trust into some of the ups and downs going on in my life.

Schiller sums up her experience with the support of the dream group by sharing, "Hard work, a circle of supportive others, and willingness to continue on made the difference. On this journey of life, we just keep going, even during times when we are driving in the dark."

There are many paths taken when it comes to dreamwork. In *Working with Dreams and PTSD Nightmares: 14 Approaches for Psychotherapists and Counselors,* Fariba Bogzaran and Daniel Deslauriers author a chapter titled "Integral Dreaming Method" which describes their integral perspective to dreaming. This approach is built upon the principles that humans and dreams are both multidimensional and multifaceted and that it is best to approach dreams in this way, as multidimensional and multifaceted. Other core notions include creativity and awareness (Bogzaran & Deslauriers, 2016). In their chapter, Bogzaran and Deslauriers describe their integral dreaming practice as one of awareness. This is to assist in human transformation in a manner that is similar to contemplative meditation. Additionally, the practice of integral dreaming serves as transpersonal or spiritual growth. There are two main phases of the practice: "reflexive emergence" and "reflective integration." The first phase combines dream reentry with creative expression, thus supporting the dreamer to experience her dream in a noninterpretive, embodied way. The second phase takes the dreamer further by encouraging her to reflect on personal meaning, spawning new insight and realization. In the end, inner experience and outer expression align (Bogzaran & Deslauriers, 2016). The authors' rich approach to bringing awareness to a dream can be utilized with ordinary or nonordinary dreams, nightmares or even more mundane recollections. For a detailed look at this particular approach, take a look at their 2012 publication *Integral Dreaming: A Holistic Approach to*

Dreams. For a survey of various approaches to working with dreams, reference the book at the top of this paragraph.

Lucid dreaming can offer solutions to our most frightening dreams. Because dreams are thought-responsive, the more fearful one is, the worse the dream becomes. In the dream state, one's thoughts are basically comparable to actions (Johnson, 2017). A nightmare, though, can be considered a gift—I know that may sound wild! Scary dreams can nudge us to pay attention to areas in our life that we have not bothered to look at. Knowing that dreams are thought-responsive and that lucid dreaming reminds us we are in a dream state, simultaneously offering a sense of control, we can respond in many ways. Directly questioning a frightening dream character, "Why are you chasing me?" or scene, "What is this place?" can bring about new information and insight. If needed, the dreamer may just decide to change the dream monster into a puppy or colorful songbird through a strong, clear intention. Additionally, one might choose to construct a lucid dream fort—one that is monster-proof, completely impenetrable. Of course, it is possible that your lucid dream powers fail and that your experience of lucidity doesn't change a thing. If this happens, consider the factors that may contribute to this issue. It's also wise to work with a professional experienced in dreamwork. Johnson has created empowerment techniques for lucid nightmares that many may find very helpful. She can be contacted at deepluciddreaming.com, and through her website, ways to transform nightmares can be found.

Sometimes changing a nightmare into a digestible dream is critical. Barry Krakow's Imagery Rehearsal Therapy (IRT) helps those suffering from war trauma. IRT includes a technique called scripting. Here, once awake after a nightmare has occurred, one imagines a new ending to the nightmare. This alone can have very positive effects.

No matter one's approach to dealing with nightmares, dream experts agree that there is something to be gained by paying attention to our dreams, even the scary ones. Rubin Naiman reminds us that "even nightmares can be a rich source of information about oneself"—dreams are critical. After all, "dreaming is a reflection of healing" (Schnalzer, 2020).

Tenzin Wangyal Rinpoche shared additional insight:

> A reoccurring dream happens because you are a bad listener! It's telling us what to be aware of. Listen to the dream, the nightmare, process it. If you don't it will return and show up in your waking life ... sometimes that demon will show up as your neighbor, or in a bar, or church, and it will influence your life. When people clear the negative from their psyche, our waking reality will change for the better. Pain speech destroys everything. If I am sad or mad inside myself and say something wrong to you, it has nothing to do with you. I need to be aware inside myself, and not say anything. Our mouth messes up everything. Instead, I can mediate on it, lucid dream on it, in order to process it, clear it from the psyche. People can get caught up in a bad part of themselves. When you feel that you are free.... Freedom is the best place to feel happy, joyful, be kind to someone. Our issues, or wounds of the past, block us from being kind to someone. Our issues are blocking us to connect with someone. to smile, be generous to someone. The issues block us from our innate qualities (such as the joy of just being).The practice of dream yoga opens a doorway toward freedom. By changing things in the dream, we change this reality [Tenzin Wangyal Rinpoche, free presentation on the Jung Platform; January 17, 2021].

Recovering the Soul

Soul loss, the loss of our vital energy, is a serious condition linked with physical and mental illnesses, claim some traditional people. Various traumas, such as extreme pain, abuse or incest, grief, heartbreak, temporary death, accident or illness, miscarriage, abortion, combat stress, or addiction are all ways soul loss may develop. Psychotherapist and shamanic practitioner Sandra Ingerman writes, "The basic premise is that whenever we experience trauma, a part of our vital essence separates from us in order to survive the experience by escaping the full impact of the pain" (1991, p. 11). It is important to remember that what is traumatic to one person is not necessarily traumatic to another person. We cannot and should not make sweeping generalizations here. Some South American shamans claim that a soul may leave due to traumatic conditions or due to abduction by a spirit or ghost (Eliade, 2004; Ingerman, 1991).

Healing professionals like myself (psychologists, psychiatrists, psychotherapists, psychiatric nurses) are familiar with the term dissociation. Dissociation is a phenomenon commonly experienced by those with trauma histories. It can also be considered a symptom of soul loss. The experience of dissociation can be described as "losing time" or fragmentation and is experienced as a state of disconnection from one's thoughts, memory and sense of identity. It is a commonly reported symptom by trauma survivors. Dissociation can be a helpful defense mechanism when needed. Children, for example, when unable to handle chaotic situations imposed on them by others (frightening adult drama), might dissociate as a way to cope with overwhelming realities. When life becomes terrifying, one's dissociated parts might not return when external events become safe again or return to a normal threshold. Shamanic traditions refer to this as soul loss, claiming that a part of one's soul is away, no longer in the body. It can happen at any age.

"If we have lost our dreams, we have lost part of our soul, the part of us that is the dreamer," according to Iroquois teaching (Moss, 2005, p. 205). Losing our dreaming and dissociation are just two symptoms of soul loss, but there are many more. Western psychiatry does not use this term although the American Psychiatric Association's *Diagnostic and Statistical Manual of Mental Disorders* contains a long list of cultural variations and culture-bound syndromes. Soul loss is not represented within those pages, yet simply knowing the concept can aid professionals in thinking outside of the box. For example, when working with recently immigrated adolescents, Western health professionals might label what is perceived as a symptom or disorder, while others with cultural competency would understand it to be a variable of the assimilation process of acculturation. Soul loss may occur due to the trauma of immigrating, but we must be careful as to not jump too far ahead, make assumptions, or view phenomena with blinders on. A final example of a cultural variable relating to soul could be how ceremonial participants within certain cultural groups may actively speak with, or even speak as, what is perceived to be a spirit, yet an outsider may label this as a brief psychotic disorder. The spiritual work done by some cultures to understand soul loss in order to conduct a soul retrieval is crucial, not psychopathological.

Soul recovery or soul retrieval is a method of reintegrating those lost parts, bringing them back home to the body. This is important because without owning our total vitality, we miss out on many of the joys of life. In traditional shamanic soul retrieval, the shaman enters a shamanic state of consciousness (SSC) typically by way of drumming, chanting, or rattling, and journeys through nonordinary reality to locate the lost soul. Once the soul is found, negotiation takes place in an effort to bring the soul back home to the body in ordinary reality. For some shamans, from Asia to British Columbia, a "soul catcher" or other magical object might be used to get the job done, in addition to various types of helping spirits (Eliade, 2004; Ingerman, 1991). Soul retrieval is reported to take place all over the world among dozens and dozens of diverse cultures. One example comes from the Sami of Scandinavia: upon locating the lost soul, the *noaidi* shaman provides an offering to the underworld mistress in order to repurchase the soul that has been lost. The spirits of fish, bird and male reindeer are of primary support (Kalweit, 1987/1992).

> "The wound is the place where the Light enters you."—
> Rumi

In the world of psychotherapy, it's a little different. Using guided imagery and some light hypnosis, I have assisted others in helping a younger version of themselves who appears confused or stuck. Sometimes this younger version of the self makes her presence known in the dream. One woman with a trauma history told me of her confusion regarding a little girl she saw in her dreams. She couldn't obtain or recall any additional details about this little girl—nothing about who she was or what she needed. This woman had come so far in her healing journey already but still felt stuck in many ways, sometimes experiencing varying degrees of dissociation. She was open to exploring this dream child, so we did a series of grounding exercises first. When we felt strongly rooted in our bodies, we cast a circle of protection, called in helping allies, and began the relaxation process. I invited her to imagine entering a beautiful healing space where she could see herself and her spirit helpers. Now she was ready to meet the little girl again. The woman was able to ask questions and even offer the little girl comfort and give advice. We thanked the little girl before parting ways and slowly came back into our aware bodies, into the room where we sat in chairs facing each other. This was enough for today, so we spent our remaining time together that day doing additional grounding exercises.

These journeys can be done once or many times over the course of a month. They are similar to dream reentry, except one notable difference is that instead of reentering the original dream fully, we create a space to dialogue or make an exchange. That can be done as well with dream reentry, however, in this practice, the only element from the dream was the little girl herself. We suspected that this might be a part of the woman left behind, cut off due to the trauma.

In Kalweit's chapter "Transtherapeutic Philosophy," he asks,

> So what is healing, where does it begin, where does it end? Are we really only trying to get rid of physical ailments and to balance psychological deficiencies? Or are we looking for more? Is it really the case that all that needs to be healed is what is labeled illness in the hospital and the psychiatrist's office? Certainly the first stage of healing is the healing of body and mind. But the second stage is healing the "ego condition." Here we open ourselves to a transpersonal, transtherapeutic level. On this level, healing is an expansion of perception and communication. The cosmos that now unfolds is characterized by the existence of many worlds and different kinds of beings, a holographic existential matrix, parapsychic energies [1987/1992, p. 248].

SEVENTEEN

Ancestral Work

A NCESTRAL WORK IS A BROAD concept and practice. It encompasses many things, from passing along cultural belief systems to ritual practices. During my interview for the Shift Network's 2021 Ancestral Healing Summit, I spoke about the many diverse, creative ways one can begin to establish a bond with an ancestor—the lighter side of this work.

First, I shared some history from both my maternal and paternal side of the family because they are very different from each other. During the talk, I claimed that anyone can connect with ancestors, even those that we may not remember well because they may have died when we were very young or because they showed up minimally in our lives. This was the case with my late maternal biological grandparents due to geographical distance and even the foster care system. Methods for accessing nonordinary states of consciousness can serve one well in such circumstances. We may meet them once again in hypnotic or meditative states or in a lucid dream; whether we set the intention for that is up to each person.

Later, I described many diverse, creative ways to reweave lost bonds with our ancestors. Consider all the things that can be done in your yard or garden, your kitchen, or other rooms in your home. Below are some examples. I will begin with the kitchen as it is considered the heart of the home by many.

The Kitchen: Do you still have your parents' or grandparents' cookbooks? Any loose recipes lying around? Did you acquire their tablecloths, cooking utensils, or aprons?

If you answered yes to any of these questions, I suggest using them. If you answered no, that's OK. If you know where they were from you can probably make an educated guess as to the food they would have eaten regularly. Try making a traditional dish yourself, if you haven't ever done so, or enroll in a cooking class. Pray or meditate before preparing a meal for them or before asking them to come through you to enhance your cooking. Make a place setting for your ancestors and honor their memory with a loving offering of food.

Other Areas of the Home: Do you or other family members own any of the pillowcases your ancestors placed their head upon? These can be used as part of a dream incubation ritual. Take a piece of paper and write on it your request for a dream visit, then slip it inside the pillowcase before falling asleep.

Do you have any of their furniture? If you have an old chair they once sat in, consider placing it in a part of the house where it can be used during a prayer or meditation practice meant for remembrance and connection with that ancestor.

Maybe you own a piece of their jewelry or one of their rosaries like I do. These can be used during prayer, meditation, dreaming or journeying as a reminder of your intention to connect.

How many of us still practice the craft we were taught by a deceased loved one as children? When I was a young girl, I was taught my paternal family's folk art which was cross-stitch and embroidery. Whenever I do any sort of fiber arts these days, I am transported back to an earlier time. During a point in my life when I had neglected these ways, I was handed an embroidered cloth by an ancestor in an imaginal journey. These encounters are common when we enter altered states. Other women I have spoken with have told me that they too own the sewing machine their grandmother used. This is another way to re-establish familial practices, thus reweaving lost bonds. Consider other "hypnotic" practices, such as knitting, crocheting or spinning yarn. If you use these as part of our ancestral healing practices, be sure to do so with intention.

The Yard or Garden: Do you recall the specific types of plants, herbs or flowers that lived in your ancestors' yard or garden? The ones I recall most vividly are lemon trees, swiss chard, orchids, snapdragons and foxgloves. I make an effort to plant these in their memory and bring what blooms or grows into my kitchen (that's where my family altar lives) to be used for decoration or be consumed.

If your ancestors loved the outdoors, but you do not recall what they typically planted, consider setting up an altar or shrine in your yard or garden. If this resonates, I hope the section below will inspire you.

Altar Crafts and Shrine-Making

For almost twenty years I have either taught others to make personal altars to deceased loved ones or co-constructed them in the community. For a while, it was something I did as part of my profession as a mental health provider. At work, the diagnostic category of an individual did not matter—spirituality was of interest. This interest in and desire to discuss spirituality is supported by my own years of clinical experience and by research as well (Harris et al., 2015). In addition, those individuals were pleased when the provider introduced the topic and shared creative ways to honor deceased loved ones. Supporting others to construct a meaningful shrine is something I absolutely love to do whether I am making a shrine for my own home or helping someone else create one in their home. I have cared for my own family altar for about that length of time as well. It has always lived in or near my kitchen because that is where the best memories of my ancestors are held. That's right, either right there in the kitchen or in an adjoining room where the dining table was placed because so many wonderful things took place there. Whether it was cooking simple meals or making candy for the holidays or hundreds of ravioli to last months, eating delicious homemade delights, enjoying coffee and conversation, embroidering bread basket liners, hemming or sewing doll clothing, or making basic flower arrangements for a good garden harvest—those are the places where the most action took place and the best smells exist. My heart is connected to the kitchen.

There are some technical differences between altars and shrines, although I will at times use the terms interchangeably, as many people do. Shrines and altars, whether working or nonworking, dedicated to the deceased are very commonplace as well as to deities, saints, and religious figures across cultures. Typically, however, a shrine is where a deity, saint, religious figure, or deceased loved one is honored, whereas an altar is a sacred working space for a ritual or specific function. You can see how these could overlap. Some people work actively with the deceased and so the term altar can apply to that, as the space may also resemble a shrine in many ways. Because I converse with, ritually feed, and give gifts to my ancestors in one location (currently a shelf in my kitchen), I refer to that space as a working altar. Others may refer to it as a shrine. This does not concern me, so I can suggest not getting too hung up on these terms. You know what you are doing. I know what I am doing. That's what matters here.

Crafting an altar or constructing a shrine is not difficult, but it does take a little forethought and consideration as well as patience and reflection. Altars and shrines go back to the beginning of time, so when doing this, you are participating in something as ancient as humankind itself. Why do this in the first place? Well, first of all, it is a marker, a way to acknowledge and remember. It is also a way to communicate with and make offerings to the spirits of special people or animals.

If you are new to this sort of thing, continue reading. Below, I will offer some suggestions and instructions on how to construct a personal shrine dedicated to a deceased loved one, whether it be for a friend or family member.

- First, consider the space you have for the shrine. Will it be indoors or outdoors? Hung on a wall or placed on a shelf? Depending on your answers to these questions, find a cigar or a pencil box or an old wooden crate, or construct a box from wood (plywood will do). It can be purchased or made by hand. Some of the dozens of wooden altars my father has made for me included little shelves—a sweet, unique addition!
- Second, choose your paint. If the finished piece will live outdoors, a fabric covered pencil box will not be a good idea.

If this is to become an outdoor shrine, I suggest using quality wood and covering the entire box in outdoor paint to protect it from the elements. Even if it will be kept indoors and covered with fabric, why not paint anyway? For shrines that live inside the home, an acrylic paint will do.

- Third, as the painted piece dries over the next day or so, collect important additions. These may or may not include photographs, items that once belonged to the deceased, items favored by the deceased—these can be perishable, decorative bits that the one you are honoring would like, and even some incense, money, or plant or flowers.

- Fourth, consider how you want to arrange them. For example, if you want to give a food offering, then that would be easiest to have placed near the outside of the shrine because it will need to be changed every few days. Also, when considering arrangement, think layering: placing larger items and images in the very back so that smaller ones can be seen.

- Fifth, now that the arrangement is set in your mind, bring out the glue or Modge Podge. These can help hold and seal particular items, even dried flowers. If you plan to seal in a photograph, may I suggest first color copying that photograph so that the original can be kept in a safe place. Otherwise, you may choose to frame the original and have that framed photo placed next to the altar when the time is right. Fabrics and lace can be glued or sealed into a wooden box as well. Once the back layering is done, allow it to dry, then move on.

- Sixth, this is the time to embellish if desired. Glitter, jewels, and other crafts items, even miniatures, can be a nice addition. Continue creating by adding all those other items you have collected, such as belongings the deceased has owned. Once everything is dry, I have laid a piece of the deceased's jewelry inside or took a prayer card and leaned it against the front. This part of the process is likely to make the shrine space expand, as it is easy to keep adding items and building outward. Considering the space you have chosen for the shrine, you may have options. My kitchen shrine extends by at least two feet, but that is because I am fortunate enough to have the space to do that.

- Seventh, take a good look at your shrine. Does it capture the person(s) you are honoring? Does it bring with it good memories? Of course, you can make adjustments. Take a deep breath and offer a prayer. Perhaps burn a candle or some incense to mark the occasion. If you plan to leave food offerings, perhaps a cup, glass, small plate or bowl can be set in front. How do you feel?

- A final word, although not necessarily the eighth step, would be to consider this space as a place to pray to or speak with the departed. It's a sacred space, after all. Some have written letters or made written requests and then have placed those in the altar. This final "step" is a reminder that this shrine, if you wish, can be a living space where communication and the relationship continue. You might even decide to ask for a dream visit by making that request in writing and offering it at the shrine. These are some ideas of how meditative, prayerful, and even dream states can lend themselves to wholeness, wellness, and healing.

Eighteen

Amulets and Talismans

THE TERMS AMULET AND TALISMAN are sometimes used interchangeably, however, there is a distinction. An amulet is said to contain natural virtues used for warding off evil, guarding against negativity, and protecting the wearer or carrier from harm. As a protective object, keeping forces from its bearer (Cunningham, 2019), an amulet can come in many shapes and sizes. The power is within the material. In the first century BCE, we come across the Latin word *amuletum*, derived from *amoliri*, meaning to protect, to drive away (Lecouteux, 2005). The following are some examples of possible amulets dependent on situation and culture:

> Vervain
> Amber
> Bronze and lead, silver and gold
> Thyme
> Garlic
> A bay/laurel leaf
> Coral
> A fresh or dried sprig of rue
> A stone or crystal, such as quartz, amethyst, tourmaline,
>   carnelian or onyx.

As Mary-Grace Fahrun of Rue's Kitchen tells us, "Amulets are easier to make because they have one job: to repel what we don't want" (2018, p. 102). Amulets can offer protection in all states, whether dream, meditative, visionary or waking. Amulets can serve as a general protective element as well as carry a unique function. One historical example is how fossilized amber was used for preventing nightmares with children. Another example could be the Italian *corno* or hunchback or the hand of Fatima, all of which are meant to provide a specific function—protection against evil eye.

Creating Your Own

In addition to those described above, an amulet pouch, medicine bag, or charm bag can be worn around the neck, pinned to a person's clothing, or placed in a pocket or under one's pillow. These little pouches can be filled with various items, such as herbs, flowers, crystals and icons. No sewing is required. Simply cut a piece of appropriate colored fabric into a square or circle. Felt, silk, or cotton work fine. Place the amulets in the center and use a six- to eight-inch string, ribbon or thin leather cord to tie the pouch together at the top. This can be done similar to a European sachet—I've been fond of those since I was a little girl. Traditional English as well as African American bags are often constructed with red fabric, however, colors correspond to particular attributes, so the use of red is not always necessary. For example, green is for financial success, prosperity, and physical health matters, blue corresponds to emotional and mental healing, purple for confidence, power and success, and white can be used for protection and purity or in place of any color. Again, these are just a few possibilities. Color correspondence lists can be picked up at many metaphysical shops or found in various books on traditional healing ways. Judika Illes' 2005 book *The Element Encyclopedia of Witchcraft: The Complete A–Z for the Entire Magical World* contains a color list and more detailed information on charm bags and their history.

Today, not only do I carry amulets during the day when I feel I need them, but I often have them on me at night when I sleep. This can be one method to help protect the dreamer or one practicing yoga nidra or out-of-body experiences. Part of maintaining health, in my opinion, is taking action to protect our psyche.

Considering the notion of general protective capacities, let's turn to Celtic traditions for a moment. Healing, wisdom and truth are sourced from severed heads. The most extreme example of an amulet I have ever come across, unsurprisingly, is that of a human skull fragment. According to Tom Cowan, author of *Fire in the Head: Shamanism and the Celtic Spirit* (1993), ancient Celts were well known for "their cult of the severed head" (p. 35); they flaunted the heads of enemies from their horses or their own necks. Celtic warriors wore human skull fragments as amulets. Sometimes the entire head was placed on a gatepost, outside a doorway, or on top of a stake for protection. In belief systems where the soul is immortal, residing in the head while alive on earth, it is not surprising that claiming or keeping one's head "was the same as possessing that person's soul, spirit and personal power, analogous to the practice found among some cultures of eating the heart or brain of a noble warrior or admired enemy in order to ingest his strength or prowess" (Cowan, 1993, p. 36). How about that for a power object!

The Greek telesma and, later, the Arabic tilsam bring about the word talisman. These are more complex when compared to amulets. Unlike the various naturally occurring amulets, talismans are crafted works. When worn or carried they "attract a specific influence, such as love, luck, money, health" (Cunningham, 2019, p. 286). Ritual surrounds the production of talismans for the purpose of infusing magical powers. In addition, the magical properties of protection and power emerge from the sacred signs found on talismans. In *The High Magic of Talismans and Amulets*, Lecouteux (2005) explains, "The talisman is, among other things, an incantation, a magic word, a charm set down in writing instead of being recited. Depending on its purpose, the person either carries it or not; it is a personal object that, in order to be effective, should take into account everything concerning the individual for whom it is intended" (p. 24). A talisman's magical signs and symbols are often obscure and this is what some have said to be the reason behind harsh condemnation by the church. Even a few centuries before 1000 CE, talismans became associated with the devil. This negative association, created by church clergy and officials, continued through the Inquisition and beyond.

To summarize the distinction, both amulets and talismans protect, yet talismans go a step further in that they require ritual preparation (thoughts, plans, care) for a particular purpose. Basically, we charge them with our desires. Both amulets and talismans, in their many forms, have been valued by people all over the world for centuries ... millennia, actually. These are components of ancient medicine. In fact, a prehistoric male corpse was found in the Alps near the borders of what today would be Austria and Italy with an amulet in the form of a filled leather pouch around his neck. Their use continued, however, although sometimes in secret in order to avoid penalty and consequence. Only a century ago, the Bretons (Celts of Northern France) hung starfish over the bed of a child who was experiencing night terrors and nightmares (Lecouteux, 2005). I find it absolutely haunting to realize that what I, and other holistic healers I know, carry, wear, use or utter today would have led to our interrogation and possible imprisonment or murder just a half dozen centuries ago. At the same time, it is mind-bending to know that a simple change in terms, from "magic" (pagan) to "miracle" (Christian), makes a difference! What's more is that a Christian cross worn around the neck is basically an amulet, as are small pouches with images of saints. When it comes to Christian amulets and talismans, the use of sacred names is important. The utterance or vocal conjuration is what gives the power. Lecouteux (2005) writes that the "mentality underlying the use of Christian amulets predates Christianity itself. It constitutes an interesting form of syncretism that combines elements of the dominant religion with older structures" (pp. 93–94). The appropriation of pagan customs by the church is nothing new and can be observed well beyond amulet and talisman use.

I discussed amulets and talismans with Nevada County local Erin Adamski, the designer of Griffin Queen jewelry. She designs many talismanic pieces inspired by the ancient histories of Roman, Celtic and Viking peoples, which is what led our paths to cross initially. Erin spoke about how these cultures all wore a good amount of jewelry and were also big on amulets. They traveled far and wore their wealth on them for the most part. She told me how an amulet is often a component of jewelry, such as a necklace, yet can be a small figurine as well. Pre–Christian societies had a variety of fun and interesting amulets often for protection, fertility and strength.

These give life to the tribe. Talismans, however, can be any kind of object, even large statues, she said. Erin specifically referenced the Viking women who wore a lunula, or moon shaped pendant, for fertility, because she creates historic wearable pieces—a lunula necklace being one of her favorite talismanic pieces. Semiprecious stones also catch Erin's attention. Carnelian, for example, was highly valued by the Romans for its courage and protection, thus averting the evil eye. Sometimes semiprecious stones were carved or engraved and made into seals or intaglio, thus possibly becoming talismans. One could see deities or fierce animals depicted. Other talismanic objects are presented to nature or the gods or goddesses of the time. Sometimes, valuable objects, such as weapons, were ritualistically offered to an important or sacred place to ask for protection or victory against enemies. The River Thames, for example, is believed to be one such ceremonial site. Numerous valuable pieces dating back to the Neolithic period (4000–2200 BCE) have been discovered along its shores. The ornate Battersea Shield is likely the most famous.

Considering how an amulet can also become a talisman, as noted above, Erin recalled the Seeress of Fyrkat. The burial site of this seeress, discovered in 1954, was unlike any other in the nearby surrounding area (visit the National Museum of Denmark for more on this special Seeress). Of the thirty or so burial sites in the area, dating back to 980 CE, the particular burial site of one Viking woman contained both the usual and the extraordinary. In addition to being buried with spindle whorls and scissors, she was also buried with silver toe rings, bronze bowls, a small purse containing henbane seeds, and a metal wand (likely a prized talisman). The wand paired with the seeds give a clear clue to this woman's power. Henbane is psychoactive and classified in the family of plants known as Nightshade. Henbane seeds produce a hallucinogenic smoke when tossed into fire, and when they are ingested in just the right amount, hallucinations and euphoria are reported, however, the wrong amount can be fatal. In addition, a box with owl pellets and small bird and mammal bones was placed at her feet. A silver amulet shaped like a chair was also present with a box containing traces of a type of poisonous white dye ("white lead" as it is called). It has been used in traditional medicine for over 2,000 years in skin ointments for specific purposes. Furthermore, three silver pendants in the shape of duck's feet are evident. Clearly, this woman held great significance in her society as seeress, witch, healer, shaman, or similar role.

I asked Erin about her process when it comes to designing amulets and talismans for others. Erin described how she sits with each piece and asks "Who are you?" and waits for an impression. Many times a clear impression arises in the hypnagogic state—that liminal space just before falling asleep. When an answer is given to her in this state, she jumps up and writes it down or begins designing immediately. Erin also referenced her extensive collection of ancient history books, so we talked about bibliomancy. Erin may just be around her books until she is drawn to one. Sometimes asking a question and flipping open that ancient history book to a random page provides the direction she needs. This informal manner of bibliomancy provides some instruction around what she is to design next with regard to the unique piece or amulet she is holding in her mind or in her hand. At times, she has not yet acquired the amulet but is given a story that needs to be told.

Cleansing Amulets

Not all amulets need cleaning, such as plant sprigs that would only be worn or carried for a short amount of time. Those can be buried or given back to the earth at the appropriate time. For crystals and stones, I recommend clearing or cleaning them in simple ways. Below you'll find some ideas about how to go about this.

In just one word, first and foremost: *intention.* Thoughts and prayers are powerful. We can create our realities by what we believe to be true. Before we do ritual cleansing, it is wise to set an intention. While doing the cleaning, hold the intention. These phrases or sentences should be as affirmative as possible and use positive language. Make your intention clear and to the point! Remain authentic. Here are a few possibilities:

"With this smoke, only love and light remain. I am protected."
"This amulet protects me and serves my highest good," while
imagining being surrounded in a bubble of light.
"May this salt water banish all negativity and be a cleansing
force now."

So, before we move on, did I mention intention? It's that important.

These are a few ways I like to cleanse amulets, but there are even more ways Here, I'll share with you in more detail a few of my preferred ways before moving on to others. First, I must tell you that my favorite substance is salt. Salt is the best energetic cleanser I know of and is used in many traditions, including Christianity. Salt is used in Catholic exorcism, for example, and salt mixed with water becomes holy water. Prayer, or intention, is crucial for it to function properly, however, the church insists on formal liturgy and avoidance of private, nonreligious usage, thus taking away the nature power of individuals or small groups or covens. For amulets that can get damp or wet, I mix a little salt, about half a teaspoon, with water in a paper cup or disposable plastic container. I gently place my amulets in the salt water, anywhere from one to eights hours. During these longer soaks, I set the intention right beforehand and again near the end, prior to a final rinse. Offering a word of thanks is suggested next. Be sure to toss out the container.

For amulets that should not be exposed to water for more than a few seconds, or at all, I will set the amulet in a bowl of salt (without the water) and leave it for about the same amount of time. I often do this option at bedtime so that my amulets can get clean overnight while I sleep. In the morning I give them a quick rinse in filtered water, then gently pat them dry. After they are cleaned, I thank them for the job they perform. Wash the container thoroughly before next use.

Another way is with smoke. If you grow your own herbs and medicine plants like I do, consider making a personalized bundle just for burning while cleaning amulets. Since I live in northern California, a climate not too unlike the Mediterranean, I grow plants that were sacred to that area in ancient times. For example, to make a plant bundle for burning, I can pick a couple stalks of lavender and rosemary. I like to combine these with plants that grow naturally next to my house, such as cedar and pine. Since white sage is native to these parts, I have some of that too and may also add it to the bundle. I place them together, lined up evenly, and wrap them with a piece of thread. I suggest using white thread as that is the color of cleansing and purity or black thread, since that is the color for banishing negativity. In my opinion, either will do. Once the herbs and plants (it's all right if their flowers are included) are bound and dry, I burn just as one would burn any kind of incense or bundle. Pass the smoke around the amulet clockwise a few times as well as above and below. An expression of thanks is again important, as these plants are working for us, for our highest good. I even like to express gratitude when picking the plants and herbs in the first place. Sometimes, I leave gifts and other times I say a prayer. You decide what is right for you. All I can suggest is that we acknowledge that everything growing out of this earth has energy and is sacred. Behave accordingly.

A final way involves making your own spray or spritzer. Purchase a tiny glass bottle with a spray cap. Take distilled or filtered water and fill the bottle three-quarters of the way full. Fill the rest of the bottle with small appropriate amulets—a little crystal and a bay leaf or sprig of rosemary, for example. Then top it off with about 10–15 drops of essential oil. I like clary sage and rosemary essential oils for my spritzer bottles. Let the mixture infuse, so set the bottle aside for a couple of hours, then shake and finally spray around the amulet above and below in addition to all directions moving clockwise. As always, gratitude is the finishing touch before using the cleansed amulet.

In *Italian Folk Magic*, Fahrun (2018) shares how she cleans her water-safe amulets—it is the way her aunt taught her many years ago. She combines water, a little dish soap, and a pinch of salt in a bowl. Then, she takes the amulet and moves it around in the solution, clockwise, three times. Next, she takes it out and rinses it under running water before drying it with a clean towel and allowing it a little air-drying time. When completely dry, she takes her amulet in her hands, says, "May it bring me luck" (*"Che mi porta fortuna"*) and kisses it (p. 103).

We both suggest cleansing your amulet after anyone touches it or even if you suspect someone has touched it. Regardless, I like to clean my amulets weekly.

Obviously, this is for objects that you will have for a long time. For amulets directly from nature, such as a bay leaf, I find it best to return it to the earth when I'm done with it or when it begins to fall apart or decay. These days, there are many people blogging or video posting on these matters. Some are similar, while others might be contradictory. Go with what makes sense and with what personally resonates. I have been taught other ways of cleansing and clearing, but they didn't call to me, so here I am sharing with you ways that work best for me, along with information from other women I respect. A final word of advice: Do not share your amulets or your talismans. These are for you and you alone. If you are gifted one, clean it.

Amulet and medicine bags are treated a little differently. They should not be soaked in salt water, obviously, and don't necessarily need to be smoked. The ritual act of making the pouch or bag is powerful in and of itself, so clearing or cleaning the space in which the bag will be constructed is a good initial step. Give it all of your undivided attention. Do not multi-task. Later, after the pouch has served its purpose, it can be buried or returned to the earth since it will decompose.

NINETEEN

You Are Your Own Dream Dictionary

I'M SURE YOU'VE SEEN a dream dictionary, if not on a friend's book-shelf, then perhaps online. Dream dictionaries are about as hot as self-professed dream experts telling others what their dreams mean for them. It is probably best to toss them out altogether, for the limitations are vast. Remember this key phrase: Dreams belong to the dreamer. Only you know what your dreams mean. Of course, there are friends and professionals that can offer possible insights, but in the end, the dream is yours.

Having kept a dream journal for over fifty years, Robert Moss would remind us that it is our very own dream journal that is the most important book on dreams. If you have been recording your dreams consistently for some years, you will probably agree that the level of insight gained by consulting your personal dream journal is profound. Dreams are not single incidents; they are a running series. By tracking dreams, we can see these episodes develop and play out. Sometimes there is a sequel that reveals itself years later. In this chapter, I will share some ways to get the dream juices flowing. These practices support further development of uncovering meaning within the dream.

Lectio Divina

Geoff Nelson is a retired Presbyterian pastor with more than fif-teen years of experience leading dream groups in churches and other settings and more than forty years of experience working with his own dreams. In the preface of his book *Dreaming in Church: Dream Work as a Spiritual Practice for Christians*, he writes about a "connection between the world of dreams and the waking world" in relation to "the religious practices of prayer and meditation." Lectio Divina is a traditional Christian monastic practice, an ancient prayer form (not entirely unlike praying the rosary) developed around the third century where one meditates on the mysteries of Christ. It differs greatly from the more intellectual Bible study. *Lectio Divina* is a Latin phrase meaning divine reading. There are four steps according to the Catholic Church: reading (of a passage of scripture), meditation, contemplation, and prayer. Pastor Nelson practices Lectio Divina in a traditional way while also applying it to working with a dream. He begins by asking three questions:

> What do I recall of the dream?
>
> Why did this dream come to me at this time and place in life?
>
> What does God call me to do and be today, based on this dream as well as the various experiences of yesterday and my schedule of activities for today?

Lectio Divina can be useful for all ages—from adolescents to seniors—at any stage of faith as well as for its application to understanding dreams. There can be a fair amount of resistance to attending to dreams within the church (Nelson, 2016), so do not expect universal acceptance.

Dream Tarot

There are many ways to go deeper into dreams. You see, for me, dreams are like tarot cards in several ways. The imagery holds a rich history and that imagery lives within our consciousness. Like dreams, the cards can also reflect past, present, and future. We build relationships with the cards as we do with dreams. For some, these dream or tarot images are considered metaphorically and symbolically, while for others they are viewed more literally, and considered very much alive. The more traditional tarot cards have provided me with additional clarity whether for a night dream or for day-to-day events. I like to consult the tarot in conjunction with my dreams. Until recently, I used traditional decks for this task. Now I use a specific deck made just for dreaming, which will be introduced in this section. My own process is as follows: After logging a dream in my notebook or on my audio recorder, I make a sketch of the dream, and then I pull a single card to gain further insight. This ritual serves to deliver a greater level of insight than just doing one of those things. For those that want to work with tarot (traditional or otherwise) or have as much respect for the cards as I do, I suggest taking notes so that later on down the line, the dream, the accompanying sketch and the specific card pulled are all there together to offer as much information as possible and for later reference. I can easily recall dozens of big dreams, but I have forgotten hundreds of them at the same time. Recollection can be even more of a challenge for other dreams, which might not have the same charge, but are bearers of great wisdom. Track and record—this is the good stuff!

My newest deck of cards with accompanying book was recently released by Dr. Janet Piedilato, a biologist and transpersonal psychologist. She created *The Mystical Dream Tarot: Life Guidance from the Depths of Our Unconscious*. This deck of cards differs from traditional tarot in the way it was constructed and in the way it is used. This is the perfect deck to accompany dream interpretation! In her introduction, Piedilato (2019) writes, "The dream images in this tarot represent a spontaneously generated language of inner experience which follows in the tradition of humanistic and transpersonal psychology of self-actualization" (p. 11). Expect to spend time with this deck. These cards are beckoning, pulling me quickly back into the dream world. The images are fresh, like no other I've seen.

The Mystical Dream Tarot came directly from Dr. Piedilato's dreams. Each card represents something she saw in a dream. "The cards came from a dreamscape, so they are very dreamy—this is no ordinary tarot," Piedilato said in one of our online chats. Many of the images emerged from 1988, following her daughter's death, through 1999, when she completed her second doctorate. Initially, she did not expect to turn the series of images into a tarot deck, but she did notice that she was being pulled in that direction as time went on. The tarot is a tool of perception. Piedilato's deck is all about the imagery! When working with this deck, let traditional meanings and associations go.

Piedilato dropped some wisdom, claiming, "Each card will be colored by what your life has to say—it mirrors your waking reality. The card is not going to mirror something that is distant and has absolutely no meaning. The mind does not waste time passing out garbage that is not going to help you in waking reality." In time, each card can reflect new ideas and memories that were not noticed or not as meaningful as when they were pulled the first time, so this deck can be used over and over again for a lifetime of dreaming. As we progress through life, developing and aging, images take on different meanings and mirror us at that moment. This reminds me of how someone can watch the same film twenty years after the first viewing and see it in an entirely new way. We see our consciousness staring back at us, right in the face.

As our conversation continued, I asked Piedilato if she considers her deck to be more closely related to oracle cards than tarot and if she considers this kind of work to be shamanic. Piedilato finds oracle cards to differ from the deck she produced. Oracle cards typically have words of guidance or instruction, she told me. This is unlike her deck, *The Mystical Dream Tarot*, which is all about the image on the card. She also expressed differences in this type of work from shamanic practices.

> For the saints in their visions or the great oracles of the world—anyone who has ever used altered states of consciousness from the beginning of time—are entering into this imaginal state and by using it, it is a pure way of saying something without any baggage. There's no baggage, except for altering consciousness. There are not rules or dogma. Shamanism carries specific beliefs and rituals and even core shamanism takes its roots from this. The specific manner of entry and journey language relates to a particular manner of entering the altered state. Thus if we call the shifting of consciousness merely "entering the imaginal" we can embrace the essence of experience which directs our focus inwardly—shamanic, visionary, hypnotic, or otherwise. We all share in

the goal of reaching this mental landscape. We differ in our approach and our rituals which is a mere window dressing. I prefer to assign the term "shamanism" to the indigenous peoples of the world, using it only to refer to it's simple goal of shifting consciousness in service of healing and understanding. "Entering the imaginal" is my preferred phrase.

Piedilato told me about a particular way to use *The Mystical Dream Tarot* for those who do not typically recall their dreams. Piedilato offered a suggestion: At bedtime set an intention to recall a dream as a source of guidance while pulling two cards. Only look at the first card and see what it may be showing you. Then, upon waking up the next morning, recall as much as you can from your hours of slumber as you now look at that second card. These two cards alone can provide insight and direction regarding the guidance the dreamer was seeking. First, take a moment to perceive the card, look at the card's generalities that anyone would understand, and then sink into another level of symbolism and association through the imagery. What comes up? Piedilato said, "This process is truly useful for those who upon waking find they did not have a dream. They may look at the two cards as a two-card reading which directs them to observe their waking life along with their current waking challenges in view of the two mystical dream cards."

Overall, this type of exploration is a tool for developing intuition, especially if we work at it for years. Piedilato added, "It is a tool for individuation if people realize it—a tool of our perception. The cards tell us a lot about ourselves if we allow it and accept it."

Tracking and Collaging

A thorough journal and tracking system can serve us the most and help link events that unfold over long periods of time. Some people prefer to do this electronically so that certain key words can be found in a flash. I prefer the old-fashioned way. Even after audio recording a dream, I transcribe it in my notebook so a drawing can be done on the same page(s), in addition to any notes. I have also highlighted or underlined recurring words and themes across time. In my last book, *Extraordinary Dreams: Visions, Announcements, and Premonitions Across Time and Place* (Mascaro, 2018), I made reference to the number of times I had dreamed of a certain animal over the course of a decade. This would have been nearly impossible had I not underlined all animals in my dream journals over the years. Make your own coding or color system for organization. As a possibility, animals can be highlighted in yellow, family members in orange, significant others in pink ... maybe circle all actions (e.g., climbing, running). You get the idea!

Continuing with this idea of first tracking dreams and visions, then producing something from the experience, you can take this even further. Collaging your dreams and visionary experiences can be great fun. I suggest keeping an empty shoebox around, and every time a magazine or catalogue finds you, ripping out a variety of images and storing them in the box. After a while of doing this, your collection of images will grow and you will discover a full box. At least that was the case at my house. Today, I have one box for smaller images and another for larger ones. This is helpful because I only bother to open the larger box for two reasons: I'm either collaging with a large piece of paper, or I want to choose one large image to become my background before gluing smaller images on top of it.

This exercise can really go far if you have a friend or partner with whom you share dreams and/or visions. Here's how:

1. Craft the collage on the same day of the dream. This can be done in silence next to your partner or the two of you can do it separately.

2. When complete, sit together, and decide who will go first.

3. The first person or dreamer to go shows the other their collage without saying a word so that the second person can offer verbal descriptions of what is noticed. For example, "I see a bright green lizard in the top left corner. It appears to be floating there," or "The right side of the page is full of antiques objects, while the left side is rather bare."

4. After some descriptive reflections have been shared, allow

the dreamer some time to take in what was said and look at their collage again. Maybe the dreamer has gained new insights.

5. A second exchange can include the *"If this were my dream"* projective technique. The dreamer, or first person, holds the collage up so it can be clearly seen by the partner. Then, the partner respectfully begins with "If this were my imagined version of the dream...." Always ask permission before beginning with this exchange, since the dreamer may be holding enough from the first part of the exercise. It is quite possible that you will find that there is no need to continue.

6. A third component would make room for the dreamer to embody a chosen image or potent element from his or her dream while the other person is witness. This simple activity can bring up emotion, insight, and new knowledge.

You might be wondering whether it is best to have the dreamer—that is, the person going first—narrate the dream. My response to that is to try both ways over the course of some time working together and see what feels best. Sometimes people prefer to tell the dream (either from memory or by reading it from their journal). For the exercises above, it is not entirely necessary. Insight can be gained by participating in these exercises whether or not the dream has been shared.

From playing with these activities and having ah-ha moments, you may like to also note those below or alongside the dream and sketch in your journal. Whether by dream, vision, or waking life experiences, these are the myths, the stories, the very pages, if you will, of your precious life.

Conclusion

IN HIS 2017 ARTICLE "Dreamless: The Silent Epidemic of REM Sleep Loss," Rubin Naiman reminds us, "Great philosophers have warned that we routinely mistake the limits of our personal perception for the limits of the universe" (p. 81). Humans have limited ranges for what we can hear, smell, and see. When we work in nonordinary states of consciousness, our perception can expand. Those who value sleep and dream strong understand that a dreaming culture is a healthy culture. We need not adhere to a sleep-wake dichotomy, primarily valuing the latter. We exist through all states of consciousness contained within a wide spectrum with many shades of gray.

Dreams reveal so much to us. They reflect our personal, cultural and even collective myths. Dreams reflect where we are on the (s)hero's journey. Dreams provide access to this multidimensional existence and other worlds. Dreams come in service to warn, heal, advise and console. Dreams become the very space to practice new skills or try things that cannot be easily done in the physical waking state. Dreams allow access to spaces so we can visit with those who have crossed over. Dreams show us how limited waking state physical, sensory perception can be. And let's not forget that waking life actions can have an impact on our dreaming, so behaving in ways that honor the collective and respect healthy traditions, along with taking action steps informed by the dreaming, bring us full circle.

Walker (2017) poses an interesting question at the end of his tenth chapter, "Dreaming as Overnight Therapy." With regard to lucid dreamers he asks, "Will these individuals be preferentially selected for in the future, in part on the basis of this unusual dreaming ability—one that may allow them to turn the creative problem-solving spotlight of dreaming on the waking challenges faced by themselves or the human race, and advantageously harness its power more deliberately?" (p. 234).

I say we can all become conscious dreamers through techniques such as dream reentry and shamanic journeying, for example (lucid dreaming is a learned skill, after all) and use these skills to heal ourselves, each other and the planet. This is not a new concept, but one that needs a fresh set of eyes—newfound attention given at this time of rampant chronic disease, pandemic, emotional turmoil, and over-consumption. Dreaming as medicine can bring us toward wholeness, offering a 360-degree view of wellness. This kind of dreaming need not be lucid or fully or completely recalled. There is no "one way" or absolutely correct manner in which to practice dream medicine. I hope this book has demonstrated that. Lucid dreaming may or may not be a part of your wellness plan. What is well worth developing, however, is a deeper relationship with our inner lives—that is, embodied, intuitive, and connected to the gifts of conscious living. Enter the imaginal and see where it takes you. This is conscious dreamwork, allowing the medicine of our dreams and visions to be given attention, honor, and great care. "In contrast to lucid dreaming, which is about bringing waking awareness into the night dream, the waking dream is about bringing awareness of dreaming into the waking day. Not to be confused with the daydream, which usually has an escapist motive, the waking dream is about practicing using our dream eyes while awake. Actively engaging in the waking dream practices can benefit personal growth as well as creative and artistic endeavors" (Naiman, 2017, p. 83).

I'll say it again. Dream medicine is for anyone who wants it. I've decided I'll take it, having given it a primary role in my own cancer journey. Living dream medicine is a way of being with only a few prerequisites: slowing down, developing an intimate relationship with ourselves, listening deeply to embodied messages with great awareness, and dedicating time to consciousness-evolving practices. There isn't much else. Dream medicine is free and it is for everyone. May your dreams be your medicine!

Glossary

Aborigine/Aboriginal: Australia's indigenous people, comprised of many diverse language groups and clans.

Asclepius: Greco-Roman god of medicine and healing.

Continuity hypothesis: The idea that dreams reflect a person's life in the waking state.

Dream incubation: The process of cultivating dreams, often for guidance or problem-solving.

Gnosticism: A mystical branch of Christianity.

Hypnagogia: The condition or state experienced immediately before sleep.

Hypnopompia: The condition or state occurring immediately following awakening.

Imaginal world: A realm said to exist beyond the ordinary cosmos and conventional world. It is more than simply imagination. The imaginal realm can be accessed through the many altered states of consciousness such as deep relaxation, hypnopompia, hypnogogia, hypnosis, and journeying.

Istikhara: The Muslim form of dream incubation still practiced today.

Kabbalah: A mystical branch of Judaism.

Lucid dreaming: When the dreamer has the awareness that he or she is dreaming while dreaming.

Oneiromancy: Divination by means of dreams—the practice of interpreting dreams to foretell the future.

Precognition: Foreknowledge of an event, sometimes referred to as a premonition.

Psyche: The essence of life, the mind in its totality (conscious and unconscious), the human soul. Also the name of the ancient Greek goddess of the soul.

Quechua: An indigenous group of the South American Andes Mountains.

Shaman: Originating in Siberia, an academic construct that sometimes refers to those whose community has granted them special status to attend to the group's psychological and spiritual needs.

Sufism: A mystical branch of Islam.

Toraja: A community in Indonesia's highlands of South Sulawesi.

Xenophon: A Greek historian, philosopher, soldier, and prolific writer (428–35 BCE).

Resources

Bhaskar Banerji, PhD—expert in mind-body medicine, dreams and wellness. http://www.bodyworkbybhaskar.com.

Larry Burk, MD, CEHP—dream tapping coach, author, and holistic radiologist. www.larryburk.com.

Joseph Dillard, PhD—creator of IDL and authority on dream yoga. www.integraldeeplistening.com.

Mary-Grace Fahrun, RN—expert in Italian folk magic, Roman Catholic folk religion, and healing. www.rueskitchen.com.

Sandra Ingerman, MA, LMFT—teacher of shamanic practice, offering a wide range of courses on the subject. www.sandraingerman.com.

International Association for the Study of Dreams (IASD)—the world's largest professional dream organization. www.asdreams.org.

Clare Johnson, PhD—lucid dream expert and author of many books on lucidity. www.deepluciddreaming.com.

Linda Mastrangelo, MA, LMFT—specializes in bereavement, grief, loss and dreams. www.lightningtreetherapy.com.

Angel Morgan, PhD—creator of dream-art workshops and ones made especially for children. www.thedreambridge.com.

Robert Moss—creator of active dreaming, an original synthesis of shamanic practice and dreamwork and the author of over a dozen books on these topics. www.mossdreams.com.

Kathleen O'Keefe Kanavos—dreamworker, coach, author, and three-time breast cancer survivor. www.kathleenokeefekanavos.com.

Janet Piedilato, PhD—creator of the Mystical Dream Tarot, she weaves together dreamwork, imaginal journeying and tarot. www.janetpiedilato.net.

Linda Yael Schiller, MSW, LICSW—specializes in dreamwork through the lens of Kabbalah. www.lindayaelschiller.com.

Lena Swanson—shamanic practitioner, animal communicator, and psychic. www.lenaswanson.com.

Bibliography

Achterberg, J. (1991). *Woman as healer: A panoramic survey of the healing activities of women from prehistoric times to the present.* Boston, MA: Shambhala.

Apsy, D. J., Delfabbro, P., Proeve, M., & Mohr, P. (2017). Reality testing and the mnemonic induction of lucid dreams: Findings from the national Australian lucid dream induction study. *Dreaming, 27*(3), 206–231.

Banerji, B. (2017). *Using dreams to elicit inner healing resources: an exploratory study* [Doctoral Dissertation, Saybrook Univerity].

Banyan, C. D., & Kein, G. F. (2001). *Hypnosis and hypnotherapy: Basic to advanced techniques for the professional.* Saint Paul, MN: Abbot.

Barrett, D. (2001). *The committee of sleep: How artists, scientists, and athletes use dreams for creative problem solving.* New York, NY: Crown.

Barrett, D. (2017). Dreams and creative problem solving. *Ann. N.Y. Acad. Sci.* 1406: 64–67. doi: 10.1111/nyas.13412

Black, J., Belicki, K., & Emberley-Ralph, J. (2019). Who dreams of the deceased? The roles of dream recall, grief intensity, attachment, and openness to experience. *Dreaming, 29*(1), 57–78.

Bogzaran, F., & Deslauriers, D. (2016). Integral dreaming method. In J. Lewis & S. Krippner (Eds.), *Working with dreams and PTSD nightmares: 14 approaches for psychotherapists and counselors* (pp. 207–223). Santa Barbara, CA: Praeger.

Bulkeley, K. (1997). *An introduction to the psychology of dreaming.* Westport, CT: Praeger.

Bulkeley, K. (2008). *Dreaming in the world's religions: A comparative history.* New York, NY: New York University Press.

Burch, W. E. (2003). *She who dreams: A journey into healing through dreamwork.* Novato, CA: New World Library.

Burk, L., & O'Keefe-Kanavos. (2018). *Dreams that can save your life: Early warning signs of cancer and other diseases.* Rochester, VT: Findhorn.

Carpenter, B., & Krippner, S. (1989). Spice island shaman: A Torajan healer in Sulawesi. *Shaman's Drum, Mid-Fall(18):* 47–52.

Charsley, S. R. (1973). Dreams in an independent African church. *Africa, 43*(3), 244–257.

Covitz, J. (1990). *Visions of the night: A study of Jewish dream interpretation.* Boston, MA: Shambhala.

Cowen, T. (1993). *Fire in the head: Shamanism and the Celtic spirit.* San Francisco, CA: Harper.

Csordas, T. J. (1994). *The sacred self: A cultural phenomenology of charismatic healing.* Berkeley, CA: University of California Press.

Cunningham, S. (2019). *Cunningham's encyclopedia of magical herbs.* Woodbury, MN: Llewellyn.

Davidson, H. E. (1981). The Germanic World. In M. Loewe & C. Blacker (Eds.), *Divination and Oracles* (pp. 115–141). London, UK: George Allen & Unwin.

Desai, K (2017). *Yoga nidra: The art of transformational sleep.* Twin Lakes, WI: Lotus Press.

Drury, N. (1987). *The shaman and the magician: Journey between worlds.* New York, NY: Arkana.

Edgar, I. R. (2006). The "true dream" in contemporary Islamic/Jihadist dreamwork: A case study of the dreams of Taliban leader Mullah Omar. *Contemporary South Asia, 15*(3), 263–272.

Edgar, I. R. (2011). *The dream in Islam: From Qur'anic tradition to jihadist inspiration.* New York, NY: Berghahn Books.

Eliade, M. (2004). *Shamanism: Archaic techniques of ecstasy (2nd Ed.).* Princeton, NJ: Princeton University Press.

Fahd, T. (1966). The dream in medieval Islamic society. In G. E. Von Grunebaum, & R. Caillois (Eds.), *The dream and human societies* (pp. 351–364). Los Angeles, CA: University of California Press.

Fahrun, M. (2018). *Italian folk magic: Rue's kitchen witchery.* Newburyport, MA: Weiser.

Foor, D. (2017). *Ancestral medicine: Rituals for personal and family healing.* Rochester, VT: Bear & Company.

Franks, L. J. (2016). *Stone medicine: A Chinese medical guide to healing with gems and minerals.* Rochester, VT: Healing Arts Press.

Gendlin, E. T. (1986). *Let your body interpret your dreams.* Wilmette, IL: Chiron.

Germer, C. K. (2005). Mindfulness: What is it? What does it matter? In C.K. Germer, R. D. Siegel & P. R. Fulton (Eds.), *Mindfulness and psychotherapy* (pp. 3–27). New York, NY: Guilford Press.

Gonzalez-Vazquez, A. (2014). Dreaming, dream-sharing and dream-interpretation as feminine powers in northern Morrocco. *Anthropology of the Contemporary Middle East and Central Eurasia, 2*(1), 97–108.

Grimassi, R. (2007). Italian witchcraft: The old religion of southern Europe. Woodbury, MN; Llewellyn.

Harner, M. (1990). *The way of the shaman.* New York, NY: HarperCollins.

Harris, J. I., Nienow, T., Choi, A., Engdahl, B., Nguyen, X. V., & Thuras, P. (2015). Client report of spirituality in recovery from serious mental illness. *Psychology of Religion and Spirituality, 7*(2), 142–149.

Holecek, A. (2016). *Dream yoga: Illuminating your life through lucid dreaming and the Tibetan yogas of sleep.* Boulder, CO: Sounds True.

Holecek, A. (2020). *Dreams of light: The profound daytime practice of lucid dreaming.* Boulder, CO: Sounds True.

Hulskamp, M. A. A. (2013). The value of dream diagnosis in the medical praxis of the Hippocratics and Galen. In S. M. Oberhelman (Ed.), *Dreams, Healing and Medicine in Greece: From Antiquity to Present* (pp. 33–68). Ashgate.

Hutson, M. (2020). Eight truths about intuition: What to know about what you don't know you know. *Psychology Today (53)*1, 54–63.

Illes, J. (2005). *The element encyclopedia of witchcraft: The complete a-z for the entire magical world.* Hammersmith, London: HarperElement.

Ingerman, S. (1991). *Soul retrieval: Mending the fragmented self.* San Francisco, CA: Harper.

Ingerman, S. (2004/2008). *Shamanic journeying: A beginner's guide.* Boulder, CO: Sounds True.

Johnson, C. R. (2017). *Llewellyn's complete book of lucid dreaming: A comprehensive guide to promote creativity, overcome sleep disturbances and enhance health and wellness.* Woodbury, MN: Llewellyn Publications.

Johnson, C. R. (2018). *Mindful dreaming: Harness the power of lucid dreaming for happiness, health, and positive change.* Newburyport, MA: Conari Press.

Jones, S. M., & Krippner, S. (2012). *The voice of Rolling Thunder: A medicine man's wisdom for walking the red road.* Rochester, VT: Bear & Company.

Jung, C. G. (1964). Man and his symbols. New York, NY: Laurel.

Kalweit, H. (1984). *Dreamtime and inner space: The world of the shaman.* Boston, MA: Shambala.

Kalweit, H. (1987/1992/2000). *Shamans, healers, and medicine men.* Boston, MA: Shambhala.

Kelsey, M. T. (1991) *God, dreams and revelation: A Christian interpretation of dreams* (revised and expanded edition). Minneapolis, MN: Augsburg.

Kinfemichael, H., & Raju, M. V. R. (2017). Cultural interpretations of dreams: The case of native Amharic language speakers in Amhara region, Ethiopia. *Indian Journal of Health and Wellbeing.* 8(3), 237–241.

Knight, P. (2015). *Stolen images: Pagan symbolism and Christianity.* Wiltshire, UK: Stone Seeker Publishing.

Krippner, S. (1994). The use of altered conscious states in North and South Indian shamanic healing rituals. In R. van Quekelberghe & D. Eigner (Eds.), *Yearbook of cross-cultural medicine and psychotherapy: Trance, possession, healing rituals, and psychotherapy* (pp. 181–202). Berlin: Verlag fur Wissenschaft und Bildung.

Krippner, S. (2000). Cross-cultural perspectives on transpersonal hypnosis. In E. D. Leskowitz (Ed.), *Transpersonal hypnosis: Gateway to body, mind, and spirit* (pp. 141–161). Boca Raton, FL: CRC Press.

Krippner, S. (2000). The epistemology and technologies of shamanic states of consciousness. *Journal of Consciousness Studies (7)* 11/12, 93–118.

Krippner, S. (2016). Appendix B: Working with posttraumatic stress disorder nightmares. In J. Lewis & S. Krippner (Eds.), *Working with dreams and PTSD nightmares: 14 approaches for psychotherapists and counselors* (pp. 251–268). Santa Barbara, CA: Praeger.

Krippner, S., Bogzaran, F., & Percia de Carvalho, A. (2002). *Extraordinary dreams and how to work with them.* Albany, NY: State University of New York.

LaBerge S., & Rheingld, H. (1990). *Exploring the world of lucid dreaming.* New York, NY: Ballatine Books.

Laughlin, C. D. (2011). *Communing with the gods: Consciousness, culture and the dreaming brain.* Brisbane, Australia: Daily Grail Publishing.

Laughlin, C. D., & Rock, A. J. (2014). What we can learn from shamans' dreaming? A cross-cultural exploration. *Dreaming, 24*(4), 233–252.

Lecouteux, C. (2005). *The high magic of talismans and amulets: Tradition and craft.* Rochester, VT: Inner Traditions.

Lee, Y., & Kanazawa, S. (2015). An introduction to the special issue on the nature and evolution of totemism, shamanism, religions, and spirituality. *Psychology of Religion and Spirituality, 7*(4), 265–266.

Mascaro, K. R. (2018). *Extraordinary dreams: Visions, announcements and premonitions across time and place.* Jefferson, NC: McFarland.

McNamara, P. (2008). *Nightmares: The science and solution of those frightening visions during sleep.* Westport, CT: Praeger.

McNamara, P., Dietrich-Egensteiner, L., & Teed, B. (2017). Mutual dreaming. *Dreaming, 27*(2). 87–101.

McNeal, S. (2020). Hypnotic ego-strengthening: Where we've been and the road ahead. *American Journal of Clinical Hypnosis, 62*(4), 392–408.

Monroe, R. A. (1971). *Journeys out of the body.* New York: NY: Broadway.

Morrison, J. S. (1981). The Classical World. In M. Loewe & C. Blacker (Eds.), *Divination and Oracles* (pp. 87–114). London, UK: George Allen & Unwin.

Moss, R. (1996). *Conscious dreaming: A spiritual path for everyday life.* New York, NY: Crown Trade Paperbacks.

Moss, R. (2005). *Dreamways of the Iroquois: Honoring the secret wishes of the soul.* Rochester, VT: Destiny Books.

Moss, R. (2005). *The dreamer's book of the dead: A soul travelers guide to death, dying, and the other side.* Rochester, VT: Destiny Books.

Moss, R. (2009). *The secret history of dreaming.* Novato, CA: New World Library.

Moss, R. (2012). *Dreaming the soul back home: Shamanic dreaming for healing and becoming whole.* Novato, CA: New World Library.

Moss, R. (2014). *The boy who died and came back: Adventures of a dream archaeologist in the multi-verse.* Novato, CA: New World Library.

Muller-Ebeling, C., Ratsch, C., & Storl, W-D. (2003). *Witchcraft medicine: Healing arts, shamanic practices, and forbidden plants.* Rochester, VT: Inner Traditions.

Naiman, R. (2017). Dreamless: The silent epidemic of REM sleep loss. *Annals of the New York Academy of Sciences, 1406,* 77–85. doi: 10.1111/nyas.13447

Nelson, G. (2016). *Dreaming in church: Dream work as a spiritual practice for Christians.* Eugene, OR: Wipf & Stock.

O'Keefe-Kanavos, K. (2014). *Surviving cancerland: Intuitive aspects of healing.* Fort Bragg, CA: Cypress House.

Park, W. Z. (1934). Paviotso shamanism. *American Anthropologist, 36,* 98–113.

Past, A. (2005). *Incantations: Songs, spells, and images by Mayan women.* Chiapas, Mexico: Taller Leñateros.

Perry, D.F., DiPietro, J., & Costigan, K. (1999). Are women carrying "basketballs" really carrying boys? Testing pregnancy folklore. *Birth, 26*(3), 172–177.

Piedilato, J. (2019). *The mystical dream tarot: Life guidance from the depths of our unconscious.* Hammersmith, London: Eddison.

Pinchbeck, D., & Rokhlin, S. (2019). *When plants dream: Ayahuasca, Amazonian shamanism, and the global psychedelic renaissance.* London, UK: Watkins.

Rankin, L. (2013). *Mind over medicine: Scientific proof that you can heal yourself.* Carlsbad, CA: Hay House.

Schiller, L. Y. (2019) *Modern dreamwork: New tools for decoding your soul's wisdom. Woodbury, MN: Llewellyn.*

Schladlich, M., Erlacher, D., & Schredl, M. (2017). Improvement of darts performance following lucid dream practice depends on the number of distractions while rehearsing within the dream—a sleep laboratory pilot study. *Journal of Sports Sciences, 35*(23), 2365–2372.

Schnalzer, R. (2020, April 7). You're not imagining it: We're all having intense coronavirus dreams. *Los Angeles Times.* Retrieved from https://www.latimes.com/lifestyle/story/2020–04–07/coronavirus-quarantine-dreams

Siegel, A. B. (2002). *Dream wisdom: Uncovering life's answers in your dreams.* Berkeley, CA: Celestial Arts.

Stumbrys, T. (2018). Lucid nightmares: A survey of their frequency, features, and factors in lucid dreamers. *Dreaming, 28*(3), 193–204.

Tantia, J. F. (2011). Viva Las Vagus!: The innervation of embodied clinical intuition. *The USA Body Psychotherapy Journal, 10*(1), 29–37.

Tantia, J. F. (2014). Is intuition embodied? A phenomenological study of clinical intuition in somatic psychotherapy practice. *Body, Movement and Dance in Psychotherapy, 9*(4), 211–223.

Ullman, M., & Zimmerman, N. (1979). *Working with dreams: Self-understanding, problem-solving, and enriched creativity through dream appreciation.* Los Angeles, CA: Jeremy P. Tarcher.

Van Bronkhorst, J. (2015). *Dreams at the threshold.* Woodbury, MN: Llewellyn.

Waggoner, R., & McCready, C. (2015). *Lucid dreaming plain and simple: Tips and techniques for insight, creativity, and personal growth.* San Francisco, CA: Conari Press.

Walker, M. (2017). *Why we sleep: Unlocking the power of sleep and dreams.* New York, NY: Scribner.

Walsh, R. (2014). *The world of shamanism: New views of an ancient tradition.* Woodbury, MN: Llewellyn.

Walsh, R. N. (1990). *The spirit of shamanism.* Los Angeles, CA: Jeremy P. Tarcher.

Weaver, C. (2020, April 13). Why am I having weird dreams lately? *New York Times.* Retrieved from https://www.nytimes.com/2020/04/13/style/why-weird-dreams-coronavirus.html

Winkelman, M. (2015). Shamanism as a biogenetic structural paradigm for humans' evolved social psychology. *Psychology of Religion and Spirituality, 7*(4). 267–277.

Yapko, M. D. (2011). *Mindfulness and hypnosis: The power of suggestion to transform experience.* New York, NY: W. W. Norton & Company.

Yu, C. K. C. (2020). We dream about typical themes in both REM and Non-REM sleep. *Dreaming, 30*(4), 317–328.

·

Index

185